Critical Race Theory and Jordan Peele's *Get Out*

FILM THEORY IN PRACTICE

Series Editor: Todd McGowan

Critical Race Theory and Jordan Peele's *Get Out*

KEVIN WYNTER

BLOOMSBURY ACADEMIC
NEW YORK · LONDON · OXFORD · NEW DELHI · SYDNEY

BLOOMSBURY ACADEMIC
Bloomsbury Publishing Inc.
1385 Broadway, New York, NY 10018, USA
50 Bedford Square, London, WC1B 3DP, UK
29 Earlsfort Terrace, Dublin 2, Ireland

BLOOMSBURY, BLOOMSBURY ACADEMIC and the Diana logo
are trademarks of Bloomsbury Publishing Plc

First published in the United States of America 2022

For legal purposes the Acknowledgments on pp. viii–x constitute
an extension of this copyright page.

Cover design by Alice Marwick
Cover images: Slave auction, 1897. From a composite of 13 scenes
pertaining to Afro-American history © Universal History Archive / UIG /
Getty images; Daniel Kaluuya in *Get Out*, 2017, Dir. Jordan Peele © Blumhouse
productions / QC Entertainment / Collection Christophel / ArenaPAL

Bloomsbury Publishing Inc does not have any control over, or responsibility for,
any third-party websites referred to or in this book. All internet addresses given
in this book were correct at the time of going to press. The author and publisher
regret any inconvenience caused if addresses have changed or sites have
ceased to exist, but can accept no responsibility for any such changes.

Library of Congress Cataloging-in-Publication Data
Names: Wynter, Kevin, author.
Title: Critical race theory and Jordan Peele's Get out / Kevin Wynter.
Description: 1st. | New York : Bloomsbury Academic, 2022. |
Series: Film theory in practice | Includes bibliographical references and index. |
Identifiers: LCCN 2021052958 (print) | LCCN 2021052959 (ebook) | ISBN
9781501351280 (hardback) | ISBN 9781501351297 (paperback) | ISBN 9781501351303
(epub) | ISBN 9781501351310 (pdf) | ISBN 9781501351327
Subjects: LCSH: Get out (Motion picture : 2017) | Critical race theory and motion
pictures. | Horror films–History and criticism. | Racism in motion pictures. |
United States–Race relations–21st century.
Classification: LCC PN1997.2.G46 W96 2022 (print) | LCC PN1997.2.G46 (ebook) |
DDC 791.43/72–dc23/eng/20211108
LC record available at https://lccn.loc.gov/2021052958
LC ebook record available at https://lccn.loc.gov/2021052959

ISBN: HB: 978-1-5013-5128-0
         PB: 978-1-5013-5129-7
         ePDF: 978-1-5013-5131-0
         eBook: 978-1-5013-5130-3

Series: Film Theory in Practice

Typeset by Integra Software Services Pvt. Ltd.
Printed and bound in Great Britain

To find out more about our authors and books visit www.bloomsbury.com
and sign up for our newsletters.

For Soleil, Dash, and Zane,
and the worlds of possibility you hold forth

CONTENTS

ACKNOWLEDGMENTS

The genesis of this book began in a conversation with my wonderful colleague Jennifer Friedlander who first brought the Film Theory in Practice series to my attention. Jennifer was kind enough to connect me with its editor Todd McGowan who has been an ardent supporter of this project from the beginning. I am grateful to Todd and the Bloomsbury team for their patience and encouragement as disruptions in my personal life and a global pandemic delayed its completion.

With a view to the past, I want to say that my writing and thinking about film, and what I understand the work of film analysis to be, have benefited greatly—in fact, almost exclusively—from the guidance and mentorship of brilliant women. I want to convey to them my gratitude. From my time at the University of Toronto as an undergraduate, I thank Kay Armatage and Kass Banning, both of whom instilled confidence in me when it was most needed. Without exaggeration, I can say that their generosity and understanding of my tendency to zag where others zig meant the difference between pursuing film studies at the graduate level or being completely derailed from the track. From my time at York University (Toronto), I thank Janine Marchessault who served as my thesis advisor. Janine had the unenviable task of shepherding an excitable young thinker who believed foolheartedly he could reshape a disciplinary field in a short thesis paper. Thankfully, Janine intervened with common sense and cautionary advice that proved helpful well beyond the scope of that project. From my time at UC Berkeley, I thank Kaja Silverman whose work, long before I ever arrived on the Berkeley campus, I spent years marveling over. Thanks also go to Abigail De Kosnik who showed passion and energy for my research that seemed at times to exceed my own. Both Kaja and Abigail served as examiners and readers of my graduate work and their thoughtfulness and input proved invaluable. Separately, I also want to shout out Jeffrey Skoller, Michael Zryd, and Joaquin Kuhn who in their own unique capacities made my time at each of the institutions I have studied more fulfilling.

I have had two close academic mentors whose impact on my life can only be described as profound. My interest in *body genres* is directly linked to their work and my time spent studying with them. The first is Robin Wood whose critical acumen and clarity of thought was buttressed by an openness and honesty that was *sui generis*. The only thing more astonishing to me than Robin's critical prowess and the elegance of his writing is the unfailing humility and modesty he used to deflect admiration for his work. During my time in Toronto, I had the great privilege of Robin's friendship and the many discussions had over glasses of beer or after screenings at TIFF Cinematheque (née Cinematheque Ontario) greatly enriched my early cinephilia. The second is Linda Williams whose influence over my intellectual formation is immeasurable. From reading *Hard Core: Power, Pleasure, and the "Frenzy of the Visible"* as an undergraduate to many years later having Linda as my dissertation advisor at Berkeley, her wizardry in knowing how and when to make interventions in the field of film studies (and her uncanny ability to model her scholarly practice in the classroom) coupled with uncompromising criticism and a fearlessness when imparting hard truths in discussion and debate have lent form to areas of my thinking that often defaulted into shapelessness. I dedicate what is good in this book to them; its flaws and failings are my own.

This book has much to say about Black life and the myriad challenges living Black life in America entails. During its writing—and while watching *Get Out* on an almost endless loop—I was reminded of how important it is to find alternative support structures in the absence of biological family. My deepest gratitude goes to Victoria Coates, Peter Karolyi, and the entire Karolyi family for a lifetime of love and support.

For more than half of my life my right-hand man has been Leon Poveda. Special thanks go out to AC and Noreen for the positive imprint they continue to make on my life away from work. I thank Erika Balsom, a dear friend and my most cherished interlocutor for more than two decades. Over the years, Erika's rigor and unflagging attention to detail have been a source of influence, helping temper and reign in some of the wilder experimental impulses in my academic writing.

Finally, I would like to acknowledge the brilliant students in my American Horror Film and Black Popular Culture classes at Pomona College. The critical exchanges and analysis that developed out of these seminars while writing this book helped me devise new approaches and find fresh questions where leads had gone cold. A special thanks go to my assistants Marco Zepeda and Lucy Ehrlich who helped to lighten some of the research load.

INTRODUCTION

The horror film has long been a reliable barometer of America's cultural degeneracy and social deterioration. The most popular and influential films of the genre's gilded age of the 1970s—*The Exorcist* (1973), *The Texas Chainsaw Massacre* (1974), *It's Alive* (1974), and *The Omen* (1976) are but a few examples—were all made against the backdrop of widespread socio-political upheaval and economic uncertainty. When asked to describe what inspired their first horror films, directors Tobe Hooper, Larry Cohen, and Wes Craven collectively cite the unpopularity of the Vietnam War, the erosion of political confidence after Watergate, and eruptions of violence during the Civil Rights Movement as direct influences on their work.[1] Over this period the stability of the American family was also impacted as men returned from war traumatized, maimed, or were otherwise affected by rising joblessness, a flat lining economy bogged down by rampant inflation, loss of manufacturing jobs, and other forms of social disenfranchisement. These instabilities find their corollary in the breakages of kinship ties and family bonds in the horror genre. With little exception, every horror film of even partial distinction through this period leans on the premise that the domestic home and family unit (or its precursor, the heterosexual couple) is imperiled by a threatening Other or is the locus of the monster/killer's basic instincts. This thematic fusing of familial disintegration and monstrosity is typically expressed through some form of repression (a dark secret, illicit desires, or an inherited wrong from the past) that inevitably must return and be confronted.

Narratives shaped by the logic of repression have largely defined the horror genre since its inception, but in films after the millennium one can track a move away from repression (sexual or otherwise) and characters who confront the traumas or transgressions of the past, toward plotlines that amplify the immediate threat of the here and now. This new cycle begins after 9/11 with the rise of "torture porn" films like *Saw* (2004), *Hostel* (2005), *Turistas* (2006), and their ensuing copycats. As film scholar Aaron Michael Kerner has pointed out, the appearance of torture porn films coincides almost simultaneously with the "enhanced interrogation techniques" of the American military under the Bush/Cheney administration, terrorist abductions and killings of journalists and foreign nationals videotaped and circulated on the web, and revelations of prisoner abuse in Abu Ghraib.[2] In this opposed but complimentary relation scenes from the "War on Terror" and trailers for "torture porn" films coexisted across media in such a way that one could be forgiven for confusing life and art as they appeared to be telescoping into each other.

I raise these developments in the genre and their related historical moments to illustrate as social and political crises shift, so too do the protocols of the horror film. Indeed, horror films often succeed and are distinguished from their peers less on the proficiency of its performers, clever turns of phrase in a script, or elaborately orchestrated jump scares than on their *timeliness*: that is, the extent to which they are able to implicitly tap into the socio-political mood of their time. Today we are in a new period of crisis as we navigate a raging global pandemic and the stunning failures of the Trump administration which, during its tenure, proved at best disinterested and at worst incapable of meeting the challenge of mitigating widespread death, slowing the acceleration of hyper-capitalism that has further cleaved what was already a yawning chasm between the wealthy and the poor, and adequately addressing what has no doubt been the central issue in America over the past decade: the problems of racial justice and police barbarity that continue to plague Black American lives.[3] Just as the gruesome visualizations of human demolition in torture porn appeared at a time when scenes of unprecedented violence and torture (videos of multiple beheadings, occupied homes and buildings annihilated by "precision" drone strikes, and bodies strewn across battlefields) circulated openly in a viral mediasphere, it appears that the terrain of the horror film is again shifting, this time on the subject of race. Jordan Peele's *Get Out* (2017) is, by and large, responsible for this shift. It is the watershed film in the genre's recent pivot toward race and has almost single-handedly triggered a new wave of American horror films.

Horror movies are often said to offer viewers a safe channel for purging violent impulses by providing a manageable way of dealing with deep-rooted anxieties and fears. But does this also hold true for Black viewers of horror films? In her preface to the published script and production notes for *Get Out*, Tananarive Due suggests that horror movies populated by imaginary monsters and demons are tailor-made for the Black American experience as they permit Black viewers to vicariously purge the traumas of everyday life.[4] At face value this proposition seems tenable. But if the purpose of the horror film is to manufacture fear and fright through imaginary monsters and link these feelings to the pleasures of aestheticized violence, how do they serve a population whose lives are socially negated, or whose lives are shaped by horrors more immense than any on screen? In the recently released Black horror film *His House* (2020), the film's protagonist, Rial, sums up this challenge in one powerful line of dialogue. Rial and her husband, Bol, are Sudanese refugees struggling to forget a violent past and trying vigorously to integrate into an impoverished British neighborhood. When Rial tries to convince Bol that a curse has followed them into their new home, Bol dismisses her concerns by telling her it is only in her imagination, to which she replies: "After all we've endured, after what we have seen, what men can do, you think it is bumps in the night that frighten me? You think I can be afraid of ghosts?"

Does this rhetoric of the horror film as a safe space for working through negative affects have the same import for Black viewers who are unafraid of things that go bump in the night? Does the horror film offer the same cathartic possibilities for Black viewers as it is said to offer white viewers? These questions remain open, but what we know for certain is the American horror film has historically been unkind to Black characters who tend only to appear in the genre in support of its white protagonists, as comic relief in the form of "cooning and buffooning," to offer exaggerated expressions of terror as a comedic pressure valve for the film's rising tensions, or as victims inevitably scheduled for early dismissal by the film's monster(s). Even in the case of George Romero's groundbreaking *Night of the Living Dead* (1968), its memorable finale sees its Black protagonist (mistakenly?) executed with a marksman rifle by a roaming band of white vigilantes, a scene that unintentionally, though grimly, overlapped with the assassination of Martin Luther King Jr. that same year. Of all the major film genres it would seem the horror film is particularly inhospitable to its Black characters and dismissive of Black life in general. How, then, should we receive a film like *Get Out* in the context of the "Black awakening" in critical theory and social justice activism that has defined the post-Obama years in America?

This book offers a response to this question by providing a close reading of *Get Out* through the lens of contemporary critical race theory. It surveys recent debates in critical race studies and film studies by forging reciprocal exchanges between what may appear at first to be disparate fields. The goal is to show not only how these disciplines mutually inform one another, but that together they provide a valuable methodology for opening dialogue on issues of race and representation, interrogating ways Blackness has and continues to be depicted on screen, and calling attention to the kinds of plotlines, story arcs, and tropes commonly associated with Black characters in horror films. Drawing connections between critical race theory and film studies also allows for the modification of theoretical concepts in ways that would not be possible were they not brought to bear on one another. For example, questions of spectatorship and identification in film studies and the voluminous literature addressing these areas of inquiry take on radically different tones and positional interests when the object of attention is Blackness. Similarly, seminal concepts in critical race theory can be dynamically visualized and performed in uniquely impactful ways through narrative filmmaking. The aim of this book, then, is to offer an analysis of *Get Out* that draws upon these and other generative connections afforded when critical race theory and film studies come together.

Critical race theory's central premise is that racism is permanent in America. The transatlantic slave trade and plantation slavery are seen not as anomalous or discrete historical events, but as existing institutional arrangements in which the principles of anti-Black terror have been extended, recast, and remapped across the infrastructures of American life. Critical race theory asks: what if pursuit of racial justice inexorably leads to dead ends? What if hopes for achieving racial equality are ultimately benighted? What if white supremacy refuses to acknowledge its denial of Black life and evades debridement from the body politic? These and other questions of similar tenor motor its intellectual program. Black subjugation thus remains an ongoing site of struggle in critical race theory and is never seen merely as a regrettable episode on the ledger of US history to be reflected upon, written about, and visualized in the past tense.

While this book attends broadly to issues animating critical race theory its concerns align more directly with the historical moment of *Get Out*'s release—that is to say, its *timeliness*. It focuses on the Black Lives Matter movement, renewed and reinvigorated interest in assessing slavery's "afterlives" and its transgenerational impact on Black life in the present, neoliberal assumptions around equality and colorblindness, the plague of police brutality, and American jurisprudence as a booby trap for Black bodies. I do not track critical race theory back through its periods of growth and expansion from the 1970s to the present day, nor do I chart its historical development as such. Rather, I offer an account of contemporary critical race theory by drawing out key terms from recent scholarship that expand and reframe cardinal debates in the field. In Chapter 1, each term introduced informs the terms that follow, and the terms that follow build off the ones that came before. Keywords in a discursive field like critical race theory often intersect and overlap as they accentuate and inform shared concepts. The chapter has also been structured with the student and researcher in mind who may require an easily accessible point of reference and each keyword stands on its own so that the reader may open the book to a specific term without needing to pick up the chapter's narrative thread.

There is a wide-ranging vocabulary specific to critical race theory informed by and intersecting with legal discourse, feminism, post-Marxism, continental philosophy, and psychoanalytic theory. The terms and concepts covered in Chapter 1 chart an epistemological path through the Obama years and beyond. They have been selected for both their significance and how they signpost intellectual developments around questions of anti-Blackness, race, and racism. They also seem to me the most applicable to an analysis of *Get Out*. To the glossary of terms provided, I add the term *trans/plantation* and introduce the trope of the *final brother* as a separate but related idea to the modern horror film's so-called "final girl." I examine terms such as microaggressions, white privilege, the Black body, and others. Each term will serve as a subsection for the book's first half, mapping out current developments while attending specifically to concepts repeatedly foregrounded in the field's recent literature. Providing an overview of keywords and debates in contemporary critical race theory, this book not only surveys, but also builds upon the work of Saidiya Hartman, Orlando Patterson, Christina Sharpe, Frank B. Wilderson III, Sylvia Wynter, Achille Mbembe, David Marriott, and George Yancy.

Given the breadth of theoretical possibilities *Get Out* affords, I have allowed it to inform both the structure of the chapter on critical race theory and the terms selected that best reflect the field in the context of Peele's film and the story it tells. This approach establishes a conceptual framework and lexicon for a close reading of *Get Out* in Chapter 2. This book owes much to, and finds itself in conversation with film theorists Jared Sexton, Jane Gaines, Robin R. Means Coleman, Eric Lott, and others whose work calls upon critical race studies to kindle debate around issues related to spectatorship, identification, and subjectivity in the production and consumption of Black film.

While the terms comprising the first half of this book tend to lean heavily in the direction of so-called "Black nihilism," many critical race theorists have made important contributions that adopt a more optimistic and transcendental worldview. But in allowing the film to guide the choices made for the "theory" section of the book, it proved wholly disingenuous to examine areas of critical race theory outside the spheres of pessimism and negation. The story of *Get Out* is, for me, a narrative utterly lacking in redemption. Chris Washington's (Daniel Kaluuya) Blackness conditions in every way the events that occur in his life; it is the nucleus around which the film's diegesis organizes its patterns. A film of utter destitution requires that an appropriate vocabulary be selected to lend discursive shape to the events that unfold. Each term or concept in Chapter 1 is its own site of contestation and arena for debate. My intention is not necessarily to enter into these debates, but rather to briefly introduce terms and concepts to a readership that may be unfamiliar with their basic discursive coordinates, and to clarify a shared range of meanings between them.

The methodology employed in Chapter 1 owes its inner logic and organizational structure to the influential work of Raymond Williams's *Keywords: A Vocabulary of Culture and Society*, but it hews more closely to Erica R. Edwards, Roderick A. Ferguson, and Jeffrey O.G. Ogbar's *Keywords for African American Studies*. As these editors point out in the introduction to their text, the keyword accomplishes three primary tasks for critical thinking: (1) Paying attention to vocabulary and how or why certain terms take on prominence in particular historical moments as others recede into the background offers another line of inquiry into the central issues critical race theory takes up. (2) Drawing out keywords for special consideration and gaining clarity on how certain words or terms developed within a disciplinary field can make specialized texts more accessible to a general readership. (3) Keywords function as a record of change.[5]

Terminology that may have carried a particular set of connotations or denotations at one point in time predictably shift and are reshaped by social conditions and historical circumstances at another point. By bending terms in Chapter 1 and their related discussions toward a study of Blackness in horror, I ask: How have the politics of identification been addressed in the genre? How is Black subjectivity permitted to take shape in a Hollywood cinema that proves time and again to be fixated on Black urban poverty, crime, incarceration, or on slave narratives? Each of the key terms and concepts comprising this book's first half provides avenues for possible responses to these questions.

The second half of the book offers close textual analysis of *Get Out* using the terms developed in the book's first half. The goal is to provide both a critical race reading of the film and to offer working examples of the concepts explored. In the film's opening sequence, a young Black man is walking in a manicured suburban neighborhood at night. He is on his cell phone and is explaining to a friend that he is lost and feels uncomfortable. When a car passes by and stops abruptly for no apparent reason, he becomes anxious and afraid. This is an all too familiar experience in Black American life. The politics of space is inseparable from the politics of race. Historically this tension expresses itself in geographic divisions along color lines of class and wealth, the marginalization of ethnic populations into housing projects, and the fear of being Black in the wrong place at the wrong time. The problem of race and space underscored many of the conflicts between Blacks and whites in the Civil Rights era. The specter of these encounters and the fantasmatic possibilities that attach to Black bodies when they occupy certain spaces (Black men publicly mingling with white women is a powerful one) or are subjected to a set of cultural dynamics in racially charged locations (violence, surveillance, suspicion, and policing are but a few) is a guiding imperative in *Get Out*. The division between urban and suburban space is also a guiding imperative in the American horror film and this book reads *Get Out* with the history of Black representations in the horror genre in mind.

The film consciously draws from the history of the auction block and the fungibility of the Black body as an object to be extracted, purchased, consumed, exchanged, and possessed. When Chris visits the home of his girlfriend's parents, immediately his body becomes a conduit for stereotypes of Black masculinity and physical possibility. It soon becomes apparent that this interest in Chris is directly linked to a secret auction being held to purchase his body and to then inhabit it through a proprietary medical procedure performed in the family home. There are numerous Hollywood films that explicitly reimagine scenes of subjection in slave narratives (I offer a comparative reading of one postmodern variation on the slave narrative in this book's conclusion), but *Get Out* is singular in its method of codifying the quintessential scene of American slavery—the auction block—as a clandestine operation that proceeds not in the presence of Black consciousness and the Black body being sold, but in its absence, unbeknownst to it. *Get Out* serves as a generative text to explore contemporary experiences of slavery's "afterlives" not as an act of overt oppression and domination, but as a kind of structuring absence that haunts Black life in the present.

CHAPTER ONE

Critical Race Theory

*The slave is the object or the ground that makes
possible the existence of the bourgeois subject
and, by negation or contradistinction, defines liberty,
citizenship, and the enclosures of the social body.*
—Saidiya Hartman, *Lose Your Mother*

The horror … the horror. —Col. Kurtz, *Apocalypse Now*

The Crusade against Critical Race Theory

The subject of critical race theory took on special prominence in the closing months of Donald J. Trump's tenure as the forty-fifth president of the United States and became a hot-button political topic after his unceremonious exit from the White House. This odd, but not entirely unexpected development was part of a concerted effort by Republican lawmakers to dam the rising tide of social justice gains on issues of equity and inclusion by Black activists in the second decade of the twenty-first century. From corporate boardrooms to political office, from the Hollywood film industry to the carefully crafted language of higher education job calls, in all areas of cultural and institutional life in America one could hardly miss the ubiquitous demands for racial diversity. The widespread support for social justice movements over this period was unprecedented, but soon race-related issues began to sour among conservatives and some centrists as coordinated attacks against Black activism in mainstream conservative media and at political and legislative levels increasingly gained traction. While discussions on the topics of race and racism in America dominated public discourse and organizations scrambled to amend their institutional practices around issues of racial equity, Republican commentators, whose efforts unsurprisingly were trending in the opposite direction, wondered aloud if teaching histories of anti-Black racism in school classrooms, or histories of white supremacy in America as a legacy of structural advantage that prevails today in various veiled (and not so veiled) configurations, was detrimental to children and young adults across the country. Enter boogeyman: critical race theory.

The decisive moment came at the White House History Conference in September of 2020 when President Trump, ostensibly announcing a plan to promote "patriotic education" by establishing the 1776 Commission, vilified critical race theory as "a Marxist doctrine holding that America is a wicked and racist nation, that even young children are complicit in oppression and that our entire society must be radically transformed. Critical race theory is being forced into our children's schools, it's being imposed into workplace trainings, and it's being used to rip apart friends, neighbors and families." Trump, deploying his signature hyperbole, would go on to claim, "Critical race theory, the 1619 Project, and the crusade against American history is toxic propaganda; ideological poison that if not removed will dissolve the civic bonds that tie us together and will destroy our country. That is why I recently banned trainings in this prejudiced ideology from the federal government, and banned it in the strongest manner possible."

Toxic propaganda? Ideological poison? Prejudiced ideology? Dissolving the civic bonds that tie us together? It seems pointless to entertain these exaggerations on intellectual grounds (though to some extent we must) or to ask whether Trump would have been able to elucidate for his audience the basic tenets of critical race theory (then again, his disparagements no doubt constitute for him its theoretical aims), or offer even a tangential account of its history if called upon to provide one. Nevertheless, the manufactured controversy around the "dangers" of critical race theory teaching and training had been ignited and would continue to burn hot in the months to come. After the contested transition of power from the Trump administration to the Biden administration it did not take long for public political theater around critical race theory to grow in chorus.

By spring of 2021, every major American news outlet had published an article with a headline asking "What Is Critical Race Theory?"[1] Among the dozens of articles posing this question some took care to note that at the core of critical race theory is the claim that racial prejudice is not the result of isolated acts of bigotry, but the result of systemic anti-Black oppression rooted in the transatlantic slave trade. The idea is that although slavery was constitutionally abolished in the Thirteenth Amendment its fundamentally racist principles were not eradicated. Instead, they were modified and reintroduced through legal instruments such as Jim Crow and other segregationist laws whose purpose was to prop up white supremacy and maintain an inequitable playing field between races. Thus, racism is understood to be a pervasive phenomenon embedded in the legal and institutional structures of America that, despite the abolition of explicitly anti-Black laws, continues to ripple diffusely across all areas of social, political, and economic Black life. In sum, the work of critical race theorists seeks to identify and reveal how present-day institutional arrangements are generally designed to perpetuate anti-Black racism and codify its operations so that they appear ordinary rather than aberrant.

Critical race theory, like other areas of specialized knowledge, is comprised of key concepts like *interest convergence*, which suggests white power (not as a faction, but as a dominant cultural formation) can only be compelled to support efforts for racial justice and equity if (and only if) it serves its best interests. Critical race theory also challenges the validity of race neutrality, meritocracy, and colorblindness in social and professional contexts (more on these issues to come), while asserting the importance of experiential knowledge when gauging the depths of Black pain and suffering. These concepts and the selected terms covered in this chapter highlight the interdisciplinarity of critical race theory and show how it draws from multiple branches of knowledge and knowledge making in its accounts of Black life. To understand how critical race theory offers a kit of intellectual tools for analyzing the difficult subject of race, it is essential to recognize that the humanist fields of legal theory, critical theory, philosophy, sociology, history, anthropology, as well as the aesthetic (experiential) practices of poetry, storytelling, and memoir writing, to name a few, are all facets of critical race theory. Thus, to make sweeping claims like "critical race theory is a Marxist doctrine," proves benightedly narrow, is shamelessly reductive, and erroneously casts critical race theory as insular and monolithic when, in fact, it is by all accounts intersectional and multidisciplinary. Moreover, critical race theory does not simply engage influential debates in critical theory through the lens of race, it uses questions of race to challenge historically dominant ideologies. When critical race theory interfaces with theoretical frameworks like Marxism, psychoanalysis, phenomenology, or structuralism, it will often use race as a way to recalibrate these theories and reconsider their findings.

Reactionary responses to critical race theory have largely proven uninterested in parsing its nuances. The goal seems not to countenance critical race theory on its own terms or its accounts of contemporary Black experience with a view to the past, but instead to haphazardly hammer it into misshapen form so that it might fit neatly into counterfactual discourses hoping to redirect, stifle, and reign in Black liberation efforts. Exemplary in this respect is a short video produced and circulated by so-called American conservative "think tank," The Heritage Foundation titled "The Truth About Critical Race Theory." Uploaded to YouTube in May of 2021, the video is a montage of disparate scenes from Black protests, archival footage from selected Martin Luther King Jr. speeches, political rallies, and raw images of social unrest caught on smart phones.[2] In the video, a narrator makes the claim that "The objective of critical race theory [is] to tear down and erase the history of ideas that created Western culture; and this include[s] American culture." Building on this invented premise the video takes a segment from King's "I Have a Dream" speech delivered during the March on Washington for Jobs and Freedom in August of 1963 and hollows out its sentiments to invert its intentions.

In the clip King famously declares, "I have a dream that my four little children will one day live in a nation where they will not be judged by the color of their skin but by the content of their character." Invoking King's words, the narrator brazenly remarks, "America must return to judging people by the content of their character and not the color of their skin." When, exactly, did this moment in American history occur when Black people were judged solely by the content of their character and not the color of their skin? Following King's speech, were Black people judged solely by the content of their character through the remaining years of the 1960s? One cannot help but wonder if the parties responsible for using King's words to disparage critical race theory are aware that King was fatally shot only five years after his speech in 1968 by a white man in Memphis, Tennessee, for daring to pursue the idea that Black life is equal to white life. Who could claim Black people in America were free from being judged by the color of their skin through the Civil Rights conflicts of the 1970s? How about the Reagan administration's War on Drugs through the 1980s and the 1990s? Maybe the 2000s? Surely the Blackness of one's skin was a mere afterthought for Black people through the 2010s. To which date and time since King's speech would the narrator have us return? As it were, it is no more possible to return to a time that has never occurred than it is to write a history of things to come.

Here the video develops a particular irony of near surreal proportions. The work of critical race theory, quite literally, develops out of the desperate truth that King's dream, more than half a century later, remains only that—a dream. In a final mind-boggling pirouette from reality, the video concludes: "Like a cult, the critical race theory revolution enslaves the minds of the people who adopt it, and the concept is blatantly and unapologetically racist." Referring to critical race theory—a discourse explicitly challenging the logics of oppression on which transatlantic slavery was founded—as a mechanism of enslavement is a preposterous inversion even by the standards of conservative propaganda.

Despite the absurd distortions of critical race theory in the theater of American media and politics—or maybe precisely because of them—these attacks raise important questions that need considering, chief among them: *why now?* Critical race theory has been an active field of scholarly inquiry for decades. Why has it suddenly emerged as a threat of such magnitude that conservative circles insist that critical race theory intends to tear down American culture, with a sitting President going so far as to insist that it will "destroy our country"? The push to delegitimize, limit, or in recent congressional measures in some states, eliminate critical race theory from public school curriculum seems in lockstep with resurgent voter suppression efforts that have been accelerating around the country in the wake of Joe Biden's victory in the 2020 presidential election. Social justice initiatives and pro-Black activism are believed by conservatives to have funneled into voter mobilization efforts to get historically marginalized voters in battleground states to participate in elections where final outcomes are often decided by a few thousand votes. Right-wing responses at all levels of governance have been unsurprisingly discriminatory. Echoing the systematic roll back of voting rights and equal access to education through the policies of the Nixon administration backed by a deeply conservative US Supreme Court, the Republican party of the post-Trump era has openly returned to throttling Black voter turnout and politicizing education.

As these developments are still unfolding it is unclear what role critical race theory will continue to play in the imaginary of the Republican base or how it will be weaponized by conservative forces to tamp down the upsurge of Black liberation efforts through education and activism, but what can surely be gleaned is that the anti-critical race theory movement can be traced to a familiar and recognizable source.

White Grievance

White grievance is ballasted by the idea that Black people unjustly blame whites for the systemic disadvantages they experience. It rejects the notion that being white in America affords advantages in quality of life, quality of education, career opportunities, economic prosperity, and treatment in all matters of juridical consideration and law enforcement. At its outer limits, white grievance takes umbrage with the notion that whiteness in America is a position of structural advantage founded on the bedrock of transatlantic slavery. In truth, it wishes to avoid this fact entirely. In a sobering CNN report covering the rise of protests in Republican states against teaching critical race theory, one white woman, without irony, explained to reporters, "We do not want our children to be taught that America is systemically racist. We do not want our children to be taught that they are oppressed, or they are oppressors by virtue of their color."[3] Imagine.

Of course, it matters little that these concerns are not tethered to the material world or that critical race theory, at least in pedagogical terms, is almost exclusively the domain of advanced college curriculum. In the bubble of white grievance, critical race theory has come to be conflated with any issue pertaining to race that inspires discomfort in anti-liberal thinking or in any context in which whiteness is challenged as a structural position of self-sustaining advantage. It is no wonder that the modern Republican party has been called the party of white grievance. Take the words of prominent conservative commentator Tucker Carlson, who, unwittingly, offers up an unsolicited definition of white grievance: "You no longer hear much from our leaders about the importance of racial harmony. Almost nobody claims we're really all the same beneath the skin. The emphasis is on our differences. That's the essence of the diversity agenda." He continues, "the narrative was clear: buried in the heart of every white person is a vial of deadly poison called racism. There is no remedy for this. Whites are born with hate built in." As we will come to learn, the work of much critical race theory centers on challenging this kind of colorblind logic and dissipating the obfuscating mists of purported racial innocence and white victimology.

Victimhood is one of the more common and powerful modes of white grievance. Carlson's complaint would make it seem that the only available options in discussions of race are whitewashing racism from American history as a lead in to puzzling over why Blacks can't just be grateful for what rights they have and accept things as they are (I, the griever, declare that you cannot grieve!), or, faced with the discomfort of acknowledging the cries for justice and equality from a historically disenfranchised population and accepting the reality that the only way to begin setting the racial balance sheet right is to concede at least some of the advantages won through centuries of Black oppression, electing to default to the utterly untenable role of victim. As if holding two competing propositions simultaneously were not possible (i.e. racial unity is ultimately desirable, *but* the differences preventing it have been systematically engineered by historically white power structures), white grievance would rather reject the notion that whiteness in America is a position of inherent advantage born out of centuries of anti-Black violence and terrorism; or it would rather perform the miracle of racial transubstantiation and cast itself as wrongfully assailed by Blacks who believe white people are "born with hate built in." Nowhere in critical race theory is it argued that whites are biologically wired from birth to hate Black people. What critical race theory does pursue, however, is clarifying the myriad ways in which institutional racism continues to exist by throwing light on the insidious methods it utilizes to whisk attention away from its calculated inner workings.

In his reflections on the twentieth century, historian Eric Hobsbawm observes, "The destruction of the past, or rather of the social mechanisms that link one's contemporary experience to that of earlier generations, is one of the most characteristic and eerie phenomena of the late twentieth century."[4] It appears that in the early decades of the twenty-first century the systematic delinking of past from present has grown from eerie phenomena to conservative political platform and nowhere is this more evident than in the crusade against critical race theory. As race scholar Carol Anderson has eloquently shown, history has always been the first casualty of white grievance. In her book *White Rage: The Unspoken Truth of Our Racial Divide*, Anderson tracks the historical origins of white grievance from the post-Civil War era to the Obama presidency, mapping out the persistent toggle between the cultural, political, and legal gains of Black Americans and white supremacy's opposition to their advancement. From Reconstruction and the introduction of Jim Crow to the Reagan administration's ostensible War on Drugs and its complete evisceration of inner-city Black communities, what Anderson uncovers is an unimpeachable historical record of white supremacy's relentless attack on racial progress, inclusion, and equal opportunity. This fact leads Anderson to conclude, "It is not the mere presence of black people that is the problem; rather, it is Blackness with ambition, with drive, with purpose, with aspirations, and with demands for full and equal citizenship. It is Blackness that refuses to accept subjugation, to give up."[5]

Against the backdrop of these remarks recent attempts to ban critical race theory from public school curriculum clearly dovetail with the events surrounding the *Brown v. Board of Education* decision of 1954; in fact, the two are underpinned by the same ideology. In the aftermath of *Brown*, white authorities proceeded to shut down schools, divert public money for education into private channels, and devise—by any means necessary—ways to circumvent the Supreme Court's decision and maintain racial segregation in schools. In the movement against critical race theory similar events are unfolding. By eliminating lessons on the impact of white supremacy across American history, classrooms have again become contested sites for examining the systematic disenfranchisement of Black civil rights. The goal, of course, is to sever an organic relation to the past in order to foster the illusion that our racial reality is somehow composed in a permanent, neutral present. Efforts to deny, erase, and forget histories of anti-Black violence, and thus bracket it away from contemporary life, have come to define modern-day white grievance.

Here we find a compelling link between these efforts to erase the past and the American horror film. Earlier I noted that dramatic tensions in horror narratives tend to center around the logic of repression. A common form of repression in the horror film develops out of parents attempting to shield their children from past crimes they or others in their bloodline have committed. As if the mere mental exercise of electing to elide violence from history could nullify its impacts or erase the tangible traces left in its wake, attempts at negating past violences in hopes of avoiding its consequences rank among the more common narrative tropes in horror cinema. Wes Craven's *A Nightmare on Elm Street* (1984) and the myth of supernatural serial killer Freddy Kruger is exemplary.

Kruger was a child murderer who evaded justice after the legal system failed to hold him accountable for his crimes. Deciding to take matters into their own hands, a group of vigilante parents capture and kill Freddy by burning him alive. Years later Freddy returns in supernatural form to avenge his murder by haunting the dreams of his killers' children. The twist is that Freddy's power in the dream life of his victims translates into the real world; in other words, if he kills you in your dream, you die in real life. As the film's terrorized teenagers get knocked off one after the other, Nancy, the film's protagonist, confronts her mother about Freddy's origins and why he is stalking her and killing her friends. Nancy's mother confesses that she and other parents in the town killed Freddy and hid their crime by burning his remains. Freddy's motives become clear: he is out to murder the children of the parents who murdered him. The morality play here strikingly illustrates the political intelligence and metaphorical power of the horror film. By hiding crimes committed in the past and erasing all traces of it ever happening, the past returns with violent force leaving the next generation to face its consequences.

It is hard not to correlate the plot of *A Nightmare on Elm Street* and the intentions of the parents in that film with the intentions of the parents in town hall meetings in states like Texas, Florida, and Virginia doing everything in their power to prevent histories of white supremacy and Black oppression from being taught in school classrooms. One assumes these parents are not familiar with the conventions of the horror film for if they were they would know that their attempts to shield their children from the crimes bound to their bloodline invariably set into motion a spiral of time that will bring those crimes back around onto them and the generations that follow with exponentialized violence until those crimes are acknowledged and reconciled. One can only hold out hope that after attempts by parents and politicians to eliminate it, like Freddy, the boogeyman called critical race theory will return to haunt their dreams and turn their nightmares of racial reckoning into reality.

While it appears that discussions of race relations have amounted to little more than the renewed centralization of expressible prejudice, as it pertains to the subject of contemporary critical race theory, these developments can be traced back to a general starting point.

Black America Now

On November 4, 2008, Senator Barack Obama—his father Kenyan, his mother English—was elected the first Black president of the United States. In his acceptance speech, to the chants of "Yes, we can," the President-elect declared, "It's been a longtime coming. But tonight, because of what we did on this day, in this election, at this defining moment, change has come to America." Almost ten years later, Jordan Peele's *Get Out* appeared in movie theaters across the country. It is hard not to position Peele's film as a kind of bookend to a decade that fulfilled Obama's proclamation that change had come though neither he nor those who voted him into office could have anticipated what form that change would take. Proffering hope of deep structural transformation in a country that has long trivialized its racist history seemed farfetched, but one could be forgiven for surrendering to this idea of hope that defined Obama's campaign: hope for greater social and economic equality, hope for better parity of opportunity between the dominant and the disenfranchised, hope for stronger efforts to diversify longstanding strongholds of consolidated white male power, hope for the arrest of ecological devastation wrought by unbridled capitalism and resource extraction, hope for an end to foreign invasion and war mongering. There were many things to hope for and be hopeful of. Chief among these hopes was the idea that America had become a "post-racial" society and what W. E. B. DuBois called the "color line" had finally been erased, or had at least begun to fade.[6]

Obama had strategically avoided "playing the race card" in his presidential campaign, electing instead to cast a wide net that encompassed as many liberal issues as possible while simultaneously championing a rapidly deteriorating bipartisan political agenda. But what became increasingly clear over the course of Obama's presidency as police brutality against unarmed Black men and women surged back into public consciousness through social media platforms and viral video, particularly at the tail end of his second term, is that however much he wished to avoid directly aligning himself as a Black politician with specifically Black issues (or to put it another way, being a Black issues Black president), he would have to address a crisis among Black Americans that could no longer be ignored or explained away. Certainly, looking back across the numerous murders and acts of aggression by police against Black people that has pockmarked the past decade, the killing of seventeen-year-old Trayvon Martin in February of 2012 by George Zimmerman can be seen as a watershed moment in the realignment of public attention on the value of Black life in America. But an earlier incident helped to establish the tone questions of race and racism would take under President Obama's watch.

In 2009, Harvard University Professor Henry Louis Gates Jr. (a Black man) was arrested while entering his home by Sgt. James Crowley (a white man) of the Cambridge police department. Responding to a report of a possible break-in, Crowley detained Gates on suspicion of break and enter. Even after Gates indicated to Crowley that he was prying open a stuck door to his own residence and going so far to prove as much, Crowley arrested Gates for disorderly conduct. In this first high-profile flare up of racial tension between a Black person and police under his administration, President Obama's initial reaction was to condemn the arrest by declaring the officer had "acted stupidly," and going on further to remark that "I think we know separate and apart from this incident is that there's a long history in this country of African Americans and Latinos being stopped by law enforcement disproportionately. That's just a fact."[7]

Law enforcement officers derided Obama's remarks, even after an investigation showed the arrest could have and should have been avoided, pressuring him into making a detour through respectability politics by hosting a sit-down at the White House alongside Vice President Joe Biden between Professor Gates and Sgt. Crowley over glasses of beer. In a July 20, 2016, column for *USA Today*, journalist Deborah

Douglas rightly points out that this so-called Obama-led "beer summit" helped to set the tone for difficult discussions around race, racism, and racial profiling by law enforcement officers. Douglas notes, "In terms of optics, that 'summit' told the nation that's how to treat African Americans and their concerns: Dismissively, with no need for accountability, and a smile thrown in for show."[8] In a piece by Jamelle Bouie for Slate.com with the tagline "After the 'beer summit,' the fallacy of a post-racial America was over—and white citizens never thought of Barack Obama the same way again," Bouie goes on to observe, "The arrest of Henry Louis Gates Jr. would become a kind of inflection point in public opinion, both setting the stage for discussions of race and racism during the Obama administration and highlighting the kinds of racial divisions that have culminated in the rise of Donald Trump and that may well dominate our politics for the foreseeable future."[9] Ultimately, what Obama's promise of change revealed is that the more things change the more things stay the same.

It is not surprising that these reflections on the "beer summit" were published in 2016 as Obama's presidency was coming to a close. It was a time to reflect back on a socially and politically tumultuous period in American history, and to assess to what extent institutional violence against Black Americans aggregated to strain race relations to a breaking point. Also, to consider what, if any, were the early warning signs for new discussions on race and responses among the general populous to the unmissable optics of police brutality against Black people. A 2017 Pew Research Center report concluded, "The election of the nation's first black president raised hopes that race relations in the U.S. would improve, especially among black voters. But by 2016, following a spate of high-profile murders of black Americans during encounters with police … many Americans—especially blacks—described race relations as generally bad."[10] So how did we get from hope and change to "generally bad"?

What has become undeniably apparent in the post-Obama era is the extent to which xenophobia and racism saturate social and political relations in America. After Obama's presidential victory breathless declarations of a post-racial America circulated through the media. It seemed that the mere notion of a Black man elected President of the United States was itself enough to bring about the end of racism. But the election of his successor, Donald Trump, to the office of the presidency signaled, in a complete reversal of the gains made during the Obama era, an emboldening and resurgence of precisely those forces that were thought defeated: xenophobia, naked racism, and overt acts of racial discrimination.

In the wake of Trayvon Martin's murder and the acquittal of his killer came an astonishing succession of video recorded killings of Black people across the country by law enforcement officers and an almost uniform brazenness and lack of accountability for the crimes committed (to say nothing of other non-lethal acts of state violence committed against unarmed Blacks that range from assault and battery to attempted murder). It would take many more acts of brutality and state sanctioned murder of unarmed Black people by police officers before becoming starkly apparent that the subject of race and racism and the challenges facing Black people in America remain just as prevalent now as they were in the years following the Rodney King beating, the LA Rebellion, and OJ Simpson's "Trial of the Century." In an op-ed piece for the *New York Times* on the failures of American politics and culture to recognize the crises facing Black Americans, Michelle Alexander sums things up succinctly when she writes, "It has been an astonishing decade. Everything and nothing has changed."[11] This is Black America Now.

Black Lives Matter

On July 17, 2014, roughly two years after the murder of Trayvon Martin, Eric Garner, a Black man, was choked to death by white police officer Daniel Pantaleo on a sidewalk in broad daylight in Staten Island, New York. Less than one month later 22-year-old John Crawford III was murdered in Dayton, Ohio, while shopping inside of a Walmart store holding a toy gun. Four days later, on August 9, 2014, Michael Brown, a Black teenager, was shot and killed by white police officer Darren Wilson on a street, also in broad daylight, in his neighborhood in Ferguson, Missouri. Immediately after Brown's murder, protests erupted in the streets of Ferguson. For more than two weeks the "Ferguson unrest" continued as protestors demanded that Wilson be taken into custody for Brown's murder. They faced off against police in riot gear using tear gas and military grade armaments to suppress the growing outrage. Tensions had already been high after the killings of Garner and Crawford III, but Brown's death marked a clear turning point and the events in Ferguson consolidated the anger and want for rebellion in Black communities across the country. Maybe it was the close succession of killings of Black men by law enforcement, or maybe it was the chilling images of violence that circulated across mainstream media and social media feeds that helped to vivify the unyielding threat the American police state poses to Black life, or maybe it was the sheer ambivalence of the Ferguson police department's treatment of Brown's lifeless Black body left for hours lying in the street where he died with only a haphazardly draped sheet covering him under the midday sun, or maybe it was the overt acts of hostility by police toward protestors and their efforts to openly decry the loss of another Black life to state violence and the demands for justice and accountability that followed. Whatever the confluence of forces Ferguson was transformed into ground zero for the swelling Black rebellion against institutionally backed anti-Black violence across the country.

Following calls for justice after a series of controversial acquittals and failures to bring charges against police officers using lethal force on a steadily expanding list of unarmed Black people whose names alone could fill the pages of this book, activists, protestors, and pro-Black allies in mainstream media wishing to call attention to these and other shameless episodes of structural white supremacy and institutional anti-Black racism began organizing and mobilizing under the banner of "Black Lives Matter." The origin of the phrase "Black lives matter" can be traced back to the efforts of three Black feminist activists, Alicia Garza, Patrisse Cullors, and Opal Tometi. Disheartened by George Zimmerman's acquittal, Garza first trumpeted the call "Black lives matter" in a Facebook post. Cullors contributed to Garza's post by adding a hashtag to the phrase #blacklivesmatter setting the stage for the phrase to go viral, and Tometi soon-after built a web-based infrastructure allowing people to participate online with, what was then, only a burgeoning phenomenon.

The emergence of Black Lives Matter and its transformation into a global social justice movement has been well-documented in numerous books, articles, and essays over the past several years, noteworthy among them is Keeanga-Yamahtta Taylor's *From #BlackLivesMatter* to *Black Liberation*, which offers a richly detailed account of the historical context and conditions that precipitated the rise of Black Lives Matter and its evolution into a widespread movement and call-to-action. Rather than rehearsing these accounts, I want instead to offer the movement's statement of purpose and to ask now and in the pages to come what we mean when we say that Black life matters.

The movement's official website states: "Black Lives Matter is an ideological and political intervention in a world where Black lives are systematically and intentionally targeted for demise. It is an affirmation of Black folks' humanity, our contributions to this society, and our resilience in the face of deadly oppression."[12]

Black liberation has always had to confront assumptions that Blacks were somehow to blame for their own oppression. Pushing back against racist ideologies that sought to enlist Black acceptance that they were somehow culpable for their own disenfranchisement has been a focal point of Black freedom struggles laboring to displace and decenter white supremacist conceptions of Blackness and, as Taylor observes,

"The Black Lives Matter movement has the potential to shift this again."[13] But where this rallying cry differs from adjacent political movements, forms of Black social rebellion, and even from past rallying cries like "Black power" is in its focus specifically on the category of Black life. At the center of this collective call to attention is not some dimension of Black life or a supplement (like power) that might aid in the advancement of reparative counteractions to white supremacy, it is, rather, Black life itself. It should come as little surprise then that the question of what constitutes Black life, and (if it matters in any meaningful sense) what we understand Black life to mean in a country founded on its death and elimination, has been the focal point of recent developments in critical race theory.

Ontology

If there is one term that frames the central concerns of contemporary critical race theory that term is ontology. In her introduction to *Critical Race Theory and* Bamboozled, Alessandra Raengo points out that one of the more radical arguments to emerge in the field of critical race studies is "that the question of Blackness is an ontological question."[14] What does it mean to say that the question of Blackness is an ontological question? Deriving from a compound of the Greek terms *onto* (being, or that which is) and *logia* (logical discourse), ontology encompasses the study of being and is part of the branch of philosophy called metaphysics. Western metaphysics has largely been comprised of the study of being as such, how things come to appear in human perception, determining why certain phenomena, objects or things remain constant and unchanging, and under what conditions change and transformation become possible. Little more than a cursory scan of recent book titles in critical race studies ("Blackness of Being," [Marriott], "On Blackness and Being," [Sharpe], "Black Aliveness, or a Poetics of Being," [Quashie],

"A Billion Black Anthropocenes or None," [Yusoff], "Stolen Life," [Moten], and "Ontological Terror," [Warren], to name a few) is needed to see that ontological questions of Blackness form the nexus of contemporary critical race theory.

What ontological questions on Blackness aim to clarify are fundamental disconnects between it and the world it inhabits. In his landmark study *Slavery and Social Death*, Orlando Patterson uses the phrase "social death" to name the conditions under chattel slavery in which the slave experienced an atmosphere of precarity in everyday life: belonging, kinship, self-betterment, self-worth, imaginative self-extension, the ability to reliably predict and meaningfully participate in the events and encounters that constitute viable living, lovability, trust, and the possibility of seeing the world as a benevolent place were all shattered in every aspect of the slave's life.[15] The ontology of Blackness is frequently described in terms of "social death," which is to say that Blackness is juridically and institutionally excluded from America's founding so completely (at least at the level of humanism) that the constitutional declaration of "We the people" in its most basic sense does not recognize Black life.[16] Social death is the abyss into which Blackness helplessly and inexorably falls, rendering Black life not so much unlivable as it is, in a kind of radical negation, livable only *as* death. *Get Out* dramatically visualizes (and thus symbolizes) the social death of Blackness when the film's protagonist is plunged into a twilight zone called "the sunken place."

The common denominator in these texts is what Calvin Warren calls "black nihilism." Scholars who advance programs of Black nihilism argue that "Being is not universal or applicable to blacks." And that " … Blackness is ungraspable at the level of ontology."[17] To understand how and why ontological questions on Blackness in contemporary critical race theory emerge out of a nihilistic intellectual tradition we need to acknowledge the profound impact of the work of Frantz Fanon. In his seminal text *Black Skin, White Masks*, Fanon argues,

Ontology—once it is finally admitted as leaving existence by the wayside—does not permit us to understand the being of the black man ... the black man has no ontological resistance in the eyes of the white man ... his metaphysics, or less pretentiously, his customs and the sources on which they are based, were wiped out because they were in conflict with a civilization that he did not know and that imposed itself on him.[18]

If ontology is concerned with making distinctions between the categories of animate and inanimate, human and non-human, subject and object, or more generally being and non-being, then, for Fanon, ontology does not afford an understanding of Blackness as it is not able to secure categorical fixity under white supremacy. Thus, Blackness is perceived to be always fluid as the categories of human and non-human, subject and object, thing and no-thing can be reversed at any moment it suits the whims of whiteness. This radical denial of ontic stability foregrounds the "Blackness" of being Black, which is to say that to know oneself as being Black is also to know oneself as being categorically unstable and open to ontological (re)interpretation and modification.

Taking this idea out of the abstract realm of theory for a moment, a recent example in popular culture sharpens the point. In response to the coronavirus pandemic the National Basketball Association restarted its 2019/2020 season in a "bubble" at the ESPN Wide World of Sports complex in Walt Disney World, Orlando, Florida. In the period between the suspension of the season and its restart, the Black community suffered a series of high-profile acts of anti-Black violence. Added to the long ledger of state sanctioned acts of white supremacy and police brutality were the murders of Ahmaud Arbery, Breonna Taylor, and George Floyd. In the widespread protests and calls for justice that followed, several athletes in the NBA questioned the restart to the season and worried that it might detract/distract from the gains being made in highlighting anti-Black violence in America. As part of a package of provisions proposed by the league, players were offered the choice of replacing the name on the backs of their jerseys with a social justice statement. Some of the statements included: Say Their Names; Vote; I Can't Breathe; Justice; Peace; Equality; Freedom; Enough; Power to the People; Justice Now; Liberation; See Us; Hear Us; Stand Up; Ally; Anti-Racist; and How Many More. But one social justice message that appeared on some jerseys stood out from the rest. Along with calls for justice and equality and reform, some of the players elected to add to their jerseys the phrase "I am a Man."

While the other phrases attend to issues related to equity between segments of a population, closing gaps of economic prosperity, calls for justice, allyship, and so on, the phrase "I am a Man" is a declaration separate in kind from the other statements because it is a species declaration. Its aim is not to call—at least directly—for structural equilibrium or the leveling of an inequitable playing field in a society, its aim means to express and clarify a relation at the level of genus. The statement "I am a Man" is an affirmative declaration, but it also conveys simultaneously an important negational inverse. To declare "I am a Man" is at the same time to insist, "I am not an object; I am not an animated tool, or a commodity, or a *thing*." In other words, the phrase "I am a Man" is an *ontological* statement and it is in precisely this sense that critical race theory raises ontology as a mode for investigating the status of Black life and Black being in the present.

Read another way, the phrase "I am a Man" aspires to close the existential abyss opened by recurring acts of state sanctioned police brutality and white supremacist violence that sees Blackness as something other than life. Warren explains how it is possible that Black lives are not only lost to these forms of violence, but wholly invalidated in the very structure of the encounters that result in their erasure—that perceives Black life as nothing—when he writes, "What is hated about blacks is this nothing, the ontological terror, they must embody for the metaphysical world. Every lynching, castration, rape, shooting, and murder of blacks is an engagement with this nothing and the fantasy that this nothing can be dominated once and for all."[19] Warren further insists, "A deep abyss, or a *terrifying question*, engenders the declaration 'Black Lives Matter.'"[20] From this vantage we can see how the statement "Black lives matter" is not only a social and political rallying cry, but is also an ontological declaration. Whereas the statement "I am a Man" is strictly ontological, to have to declare that "Black lives matter" operates both as a moniker for a specific constellation of political, ideological, and social grassroots activism that takes up the defense of Black life (particularly from the position of Black Feminism), *and* as an ontological statement for what it takes as its object is Black life itself.

Afropessimism

In recent years, ontological questions around anti-Blackness and Black life have consolidated under the banner of Afropessimism. A technical term developing out of recent academic debate informed by earlier work from race scholars like Fanon, Patterson, Cornel West, Lewis Gordon, and Saidiya Hartman, Afropessimism is a portmanteau of "African" and "pessimism," and as its chief proponent Frank B. Wilderson III claims, "it is a theoretical lens that clarifies the irreconcilable differences between, on the one hand, the violence of capitalism, gender oppression, and White supremacy ... and, on the other hand, the violence of anti-Blackness."[21] Taken in the context of Warren's insistence that Blackness is ontologically terrifying because it is a constant confrontation with, to put it somewhat convolutedly, a non-existing existent (Blackness), Afropessimism can be thought of as an attempt to theorize that "ontological terror" and to provide critical scaffolding for work of similar "pessimistic" disposition.

The central premise of Afropessimism is that: "Blackness is coterminous with Slaveness. Blackness *is* social death, which is to say that there was never a prior moment of plenitude, never a moment of equilibrium, never a moment of social life. Blackness, as a paradigmatic position (rather than an ensemble of identities, cultural practices, or anthropological accoutrements), cannot be disimbricated from slavery."[22] To insist that Blackness and slaveness are one and cannot be made separate or thought apart is, understatedly, a radical claim. Here the ontological dimensions of Afropessimism come into view. If Blackness and slaveness are constitutively one then to be Black even in the present is to occupy, in a fundamental way, the interstice between being and thing. In his essay "Afropessimism: The Unclear Word," critical race theorist Jared Sexton elucidates the stakes of Afropessimism and its radical sensibilities when he asks, "What is the nature of a form of being that presents a problem for the thought of being itself? More precisely, what is the nature of a human being whose human being is put into question radically and by definition, a human being whose being human raises the question of human being at all?"[23]

Afropessimism names the vertiginous realization that anti-Blackness does not seek, nor does it desire the absence of Blackness from the world because, as it turns out, the rejuvenation and renewal of whiteness is dependent upon the destruction of Blackness and thus requires that Blackness be made perpetually available to be broken and disintegrated. From the perspective of Black consciousness to arrive at the thought that "Blacks are not Human subjects, but are instead structurally inert props, implements for the execution of White and non-Black fantasies and sadomasochistic pleasures," is to have to confront the fact that the category of "Human" does not apply to Blacks in any meaningful sense of the word.[24] What then do we make of structural violence committed against Black people that appears overarchingly eliminative in its design, frequency and in its aims, but is in fact utterly dependent on the presence of Blackness so that it may be shattered and its pieces used to compose a fantasmatic mural of its own plenitude?

In the opening pages of his book *Afropessimism*, Wilderson offers a personal account of the moment he realized what it meant to be an Afropessimist. He experiences a psychotic episode one evening after looking into a bathroom mirror at his reflection and reciting to himself these lines of poetry:

> *for Halloween I washed my*
> *face and wore my*
> *school clothes went door to*
> *door as a nightmare.*

Wilderson describes being "overcome by vertigo" as he stumbled from his apartment to a nearby clinic where, upon arrival, voiceless and convulsed by sobs, a doctor and nurse try to ascertain what ails him. When he regains sufficient enough composure to speak, Wilderson explains to the medics that his episode was brought on by the stress of graduate school. While not entirely untrue, Wilderson admits that in reality: "I couldn't tell them … that my breakdown was brought on by a breakthrough, one in which I finally understood why I was too black for care."[25] Where he had previously been able to analogize Black suffering in the context of other subaltern struggles with friends and allies such as Palestinians, Native Americans, and the working class, Wilderson rather dramatically comes to a realization that will shape the contours of Afropessimism: Black suffering is singular in its isolation from any possible narrative of redemption and thus cannot be analogized with any other historical instances of racial violence and oppression in which redemption is even remotely conceivable.[26] As he argues throughout his book, Afropessimism "provides a theoretical apparatus that allows Black people to *not* have to be burdened by the ruse of analogy—because analogy mystifies, rather than clarifies, Black suffering … It is pessimistic about the claims theories of liberation make when these theories try to explain Black suffering or when they analogize Black suffering with the suffering of other oppressed beings."[27]

Though Afropessimism and its practitioners seek to provide a theoretical lens that brings the many facets of the afterlives of slavery and the pervasive forms it takes in present-day Black life into focus, there is ample precedent for the nihilistic sensibilities guiding its theoretical orientations. In his review of Wilderson's *Afropessimism*, race scholar Jesse McCarthy rightly points out that "Racial exceptionalism, political immutability, 'antiblackness' as structural antagonism, and abjection in the form of 'social death': each of these concepts predates Afropessimism, and ... together they form its foundation."[28] Thus, this so-called pessimistic approach to thinking through the troubling questions of Blackness is not unique to Afropessimism, nor is its focus on the ontological issues that any serious critical race work raises (or should raise), but as McCarthy argues, " ... it is the synthesis of all these ideas into one purportedly coherent worldview that [is] the innovation of Afropessimism."[29] While I agree with McCarthy that Afropessimism distinguishes itself as a mode of inquiry in contemporary critical race theory by uniting some of the most important developments in Black thought in the latter half of the twentieth century, its real innovation may have less to do with its combinatory power than with its concentration and intensification of the nihilistic dimensions of the aforementioned concepts from which it emerges.

"Afropessimism helps us understand why the violence that saturates Black life isn't threatened with elimination just because it is exposed," writes Wilderson.[30] What he calls the ruse of analogy, Taylor might argue actually deepens "the cleavages between groups that would otherwise have every interest in combining forces."[31] If the phrase "Black Lives Matter" is the rallying cry around which protests for social justice and equity gravitate, one of the purposes of contemporary critical race theory is to illustrate that the history of America and all of the institutions on which it is founded and maintained show time and again that it is not a given that Black life matters.

It would seem Afropessimism (Black nihilism) and the tenets of the Black Lives Matter movement appear to offer conflicting ideological views. However, they are in fact closely related in fundamentally nihilistic ways and between their opposing poles they form an influential axis that runs through critical race theory. How do we reconcile the opposing views that Black life matters and that Black life does not matter so that their theoretical compatibilities can be brought into focus?

One can reasonably presume that the phrase "Black Lives Matter" and the social and political efforts it mobilizes seek to prove its statement true: Black life matters. But to have to insist that a life matters presupposes a condition of possibility exists in which that life does not matter, and so the value of that life must be actively secured against its not mattering. The Black Lives Matter movement, then, can be viewed as optimistic— at least ideologically—in its approach to affirming Black life against racial antagonism. On the other hand, the theoretical lens of Afropessimism argues that the violence perpetrated against Black people is,

> ... not a form of discrimination; it is a necessary violence; a health tonic for everyone who is not Black; an ensemble of sadistic rituals and captivity that could only happen to a sentient being in one of two circumstances: a person has broken the law, which is to say, cracked out of turn given the rules that govern; or the person is a slave, which is to say, no prerequisites are required for an act of brutality to be incurred.[32]

While the objectives of Afropessimism and Black Lives Matter may appear to contradict one another, when combined and contrasted they in fact throw light on the central problem of contemporary critical race theory: how do we fight for the value of Black life in a world where Black life would appear not to matter? To be clear, Afropessimism does not claim that Black life does not matter *in toto*. To repeat its more radical proposition: Black life matters—it matters very much—but only insofar as it is needed for the renewal and regeneration of white supremacy or other oppressed groups that seek to throw into relief their own subjugated status when contrasted with the plight of Black people. The Black Lives Matter movement insists Black life matters, but as Warren and others emphatically argue, to have to declare, "Black lives matter" is to immediately face the possibility that Black life does not matter, for if it did it would not be necessary to assert that "Black life matters." To more cogently make the point we need only invert the modifying term. Take the statement "white lives matter." The content of the phrase is so patently evident as to be utterly absurd to declare at all. So, while it is true that what is implied by the Black Lives Matter movement are life-affirming gains, there is something inherently negational in having to actively and openly affirm Black life mattering in the first place.

This is the problem of the social death of Blackness. It is also, as we will see in Chapter 2, the central dilemma in *Get Out*. While this drama does play out at the scale of life or death with alarming frequency, more often it takes muted and subtle forms that require close reading and unpacking. To understand how Chris Washington and the other Black characters experience these subtle forms of racial antagonism in *Get Out* we will first need to identify some of its prevailing forms.

Microaggressions

The term "microaggression" is used to describe subtle and covert forms of racism that typically appear to be unintentional or result from ignorance or insensitivity on the part of the perpetrator. It is another way in which white power, denial, hegemony, and privilege are articulated through processes by which the Black body and Black being are interpellated. Microaggressions are seemingly innocuous, therefore condemning microaggressive events remains risky and uncertain for Black people because the perpetrators often do not realize they are engaging in racially discriminatory actions. The OED defines microaggressions as: "A statement, action, or incident regarded as an instance of indirect, subtle, or unintentional discrimination or prejudice against members of a marginalized group such as a racial minority."[33] While true, this definition misses some important nuance. If we direct our attention less toward the microaggressive event or incident alone and pay closer attention to the social and historical conditions that make forms of invalidation, insult, and disrespect permissible, we can see how microaggressions merely index longstanding structures of racism and prejudice.

Microaggressions are not necessarily difficult to detect, but as they are frequently folded into everyday encounters through "innocent" remarks, humor in poor taste, or observations and opinions couched in ignorance, they often provoke energy-depleting calculations and assessments on the part of Black people who must determine if a questionable moment or episode is racially inflected. Author Ijeoma Oluo describes microaggressions as "small daily insults ... perpetrated against marginalized or oppressed people because of their affiliation with that marginalized or oppressed group ... ."[34] Oluo offers some everyday examples of microaggressions that include phrases like "That's so ghetto," "You don't sound black," and "Excuse me, this is the first-class area." Other examples include when a white person or non-Black person of color uses the term "baby daddy" ironically, or we might recall white golfer Fuzzy Zoeller's remarks in 1997 when asked to comment on the remarkable play of a then twenty-one-year old Tiger Woods who was on the cusp of winning his first Master's golf tournament: "You pat him on the back and say congratulations and enjoy it and tell him not to serve fried chicken next year. Got it. Or collard greens or whatever the hell they serve."[35]

Psychologist Derald Wing Sue describes microaggressions as "the brief and commonplace daily verbal, behavioral, and environmental indignities, whether intentional or unintentional, that communicate hostile, derogatory, or negative racial, gender, and sexual orientation, and religious slights and insults to the target person or group."[36] In his pathbreaking research, Sue argues that microaggressions have four distinct qualities:

1 Microaggressions can be easily explained away (a misunderstanding or a mistake).

2 Microaggressions are cumulative.

3 Microaggressions are perpetrated by many different people.

4 Many people do not consciously know they are perpetrating a microaggression against someone.

Sue also suggests that there are five domains of microaggressive events: *incident, perception, reaction, interpretation,* and *consequence.* Microaggressions are expressed not only through words but also through actions that, again, on the face of things would appear not to be explicitly racist, but are freighted with discrimination.

Philosopher George Yancy powerfully encapsulates the feeling of being Black and experiencing microaggressions in his descriptions of walking behind a white person on an empty sidewalk and feeling the need to cross the street to preserve their comfort, or walking through a parking lot and hearing the sound of car doors locking or windows rolling up as you approach: "Through an uneventful, mundane act of white index fingers locking a car door or a white hand rolling up a car window, the color line is drawn, a boundary is created."[37] If we fold Yancy's example into Sue's model, the *incident* here is an environmental situation that expresses a constructed tension between a Black body and its proximity to closed off white spaces through a behavioral pattern of doors locking with the sound of a click. The *perception* of the event (the Black person's belief that an incident is racially charged) develops out of repeated exposure to this pattern. Yancy describes it as "clicks that install." He decodes the meaning behind the clicking sounds of car doors locking in response to his spatial proximity as: "*Click* (violent), *Click* (sexually rapacious), *Click* (primitive), *Click* (inferior), *Click* (unreliable), *Click* (shiftless), *Click* (gang-banger), *Click* (malevolent), *Click* (evil)."[38] The perception of this incident is that the sound of the door locks clicking (over and over again) is racially charged and that it is Blackness and the Black body itself through no cause of its own that automatically triggers this response.

Being Black and being exposed to conditions under which one's Blackness is indirectly and, in many cases, unintentionally foregrounded in a negative light can lead to *reactions* that include skepticism, paranoia, cautiousness, and doubting one's own sanity. In the context of Yancy's example it leads one to ask questions like "Are the doors locking because of me?" "Do I seem scary?" "Do they think I'm really going to walk over and get inside their car?" Over time these reactions may also turn into statements of self-validation like "I'm a successful Black person, how dare they think I'm going to rob them"; or "You're probably more likely to rob me than I am you! You seeing me and locking your door is absurd." And yet another reaction that may develop out of weariness from exposure to hearing doors lock as a Black person moving through worlds of white privilege is explaining away the incidents and chalking them up to ignorance or simply white people not knowing any better. But these forms of excuse-making and equivocation only serve to embed more deeply one's racialized status in a society that perceives one automatically to be threatening.

As a Black person hearing these clicks repeatedly, you are left to *interpret* them and what they signify (concern for safety, protection against possible threat, being in proximity to danger). As Yancy insists, "The clicks are *doing something*. My body is circumscribed as a site of danger. From the perspective of whiteness, the clicks are necessary for the heinous acts that I will perform by virtue of my blackness."[39] The Black person who hears these *clicks* is left to interpret the situation as "you don't belong," "you are abnormal," you are inferior," "you are all the same." Of course, the irony here is that if the Black person experiencing the microaggression were to ask the white person locking their door if they were doing so on account of their being Black, out of fear of being perceived as racist, the response would likely be a vehement dismissal of any such suggestion (they might even go so far as to declare that they are *colorblind!*), leading to more effort being expended on the part of the Black person left to validate white self-assessments of anti-racism ("Of course you're not racist. I'm sure you have Black friends. You were just locking your car door; really, it's fine").

Finally, the *consequences* that arise from the cumulative clicks, Yancy says, "… begins to fragment my existence and cut away at my integrity."[40] Though he does not refer to these incidents as microaggressions, we can draw similarities to what Oluo describes as the psychological damage done by "the cumulative effect of these constant reminders that you are 'less than.'"[41] As Sue notes, one is left feeling a sense of powerlessness, invisibility, and feeling pressed to invent coping strategies as a way of navigating an everyday world in which microaggressions are commonplace. As Lauren Berlant suggests, "the concept of the 'microaggression' had to be invented to create a disagreement about whether events that happen between people are specific to the unique situation or are general expressions of structural inequality. Of course the answer is always both."[42]

In the following chapter we will see how *Get Out* is not just a horror film that is exemplary of how microaggressions occur, what forms they take, and the impact they have on Black consciousness, but also illustrates how the "unique situations" in which Chris is microaggressed accumulate to form a composite image of the structural inequality that makes "soft racism" permissible. As Sue, Capodilupo, and Holder put it, "Microaggressions inevitably produce a clash of racial realities where the experiences of racism by Blacks are pitted against the views of Whites who hold the power to define the situation in nonracial terms."[43]

White Privilege

Privilege holds both positive and negative connotations. In the former sense it is deployed as an expression of gratitude for a possession, an opportunity, or access to resources that better one's life. In the latter sense it describes advantages (earned and unearned) that make sustaining life and enjoyment, setting and achieving goals, and maintaining contentment easier for some than it is for others. To distinguish these senses of privilege visibility is key for one can only gauge their advantages if the disadvantages of others are measurably known. When privilege is attached to a particular group or segment of the population it describes social, political, or economic asymmetries between them and their relations to others. White privilege encapsulates these asymmetries in their fullest possible sense.

In *Critical Race Theory: An Introduction*, Richard Delgado and Jean Stefancic describe white privilege as the myriad social advantages and benefits that come with being a member of a dominant race. It names processes by which "white people benefit from a system of favors, exchanges and courtesies from which outsiders of color are frequently excluded."[44] White privilege appears on the scene when whiteness proves ignorant of its inherent advantages or when it holds fast to the fiction that the playing field is level and race does not factor into the composition of the world around it. As it turns out, some of the most influential and widely circulated accounts of white privilege have come not from Black or brown writers who describe its causes, consequences, or who relay its effects firsthand. They have come instead, somewhat ironically, from white antiracist thinkers.

In his book, *White Like Me: Reflections of Race From a Privileged Son*, Tim Wise recounts occasions in his early life when the privilege his whiteness affords became apparent to him. He describes encounters with other well-meaning white people who would engage in activities or make choices that, while not overtly racist or anti-Black, profited from or were made possible by systems of Black oppression. What Wise comes to discover is that, despite experiences with class discrimination and the economic hurdles he and his family faced while he was growing up, his whiteness—a thing conferred automatically like a crown from monarch to first-born son—afforded him advantages and freedoms so seamlessly woven into the fabric of his everyday life that it would require close, sustained inspection over years to make them apparent.

In *White Fragility*, Robin Diangelo describes the difficulty of coming to accept the reality that she has profited from systems of Black exclusion and how her whiteness structurally implicates her despite a conscious opposition to racist views and practices. She describes growing into an awareness of how the concept of racism among progressive, well-meaning white people is always something objectively outside of themselves. She also notes the fierce objections raised when progressive whites are implicated in racist activities or identified as agents, however unwittingly, perpetuating systems of white power that hinge on racial oppression. As Diangelo writes, "Personal reflections on my own racism, a more critical view of media and other aspects of culture, and exposure to the perspectives of [mentors of color] all helped me to see how ... pillars of racism worked."[45]

In her celebrated "privilege papers," Peggy Mcintosh similarly describes coming into an awareness of white privilege while in the company of progressive white men who had joined a feminist working group. In these encounters with "good men" who obliviously were apt to make remarks marginalizing the very group they had come to work and advocate on behalf of, Mcintosh learned through these exertions of gender privilege that she too may also be oblivious to her own unwitting enactments of racial privilege. She writes, "I have come to see white privilege as an invisible package of unearned assets that I can count on cashing in each day, but about which I was 'meant' to remain oblivious." This obliviousness is a critical feature of white privilege. White privilege, like other forms of structured privilege, works best when it simply appears to be the norm.

In these three separate though similar accounts of white privilege by white people their self-reflections are epiphanic in tone as dawn breaks on a vista of racial discovery, making suddenly visible a world of inherent advantages and entitlements, leaving the writers to offer descriptions of their new found commitments to individual transformation and accountability on issues of race. These are all accounts in which white people, to use a term to come later in this chapter, become "woke" to their privilege, but, ultimately, the most powerful dimension of white privilege is simply not having to speak about it, place into the greater context of a co-inhabited world, interrogate, or be concerned with "whiteness" or consider the affordances it endows. While being white means never having to think about race, often whiteness *knows* its privilege and deliberately abuses it. This is white privilege in its most insidious form. The following incident is exemplary of a white person who is aware of the "knapsack" in their possession and who has a full accounting of its inventory, all of which is accessible and always at the ready.

On May 25, 2020, Amy Cooper, a white woman, was confronted by a Black birdwatcher, Christian Cooper (no relation), who asked Amy to leash her dog as required by law in a section of New York's Central Park known as The Ramble. A. Cooper refused to comply with C. Cooper's request, sparking a heated dispute. In response to C. Cooper's request that she leash her dog, A. Cooper called 911 from her cell phone and declared to emergency dispatch in a faux-hysterical tone that "An African-American man is threatening my life." This, even though C. Cooper was video recording the incident with his mobile phone and standing roughly ten feet away from her. Amy, aware of her white privilege and the near immutable power it confers, knew that if the police arrived, they would likely absolve her of any wrongdoing and presume Christian guilty (of what, is irrelevant) without any questions. In threatening C. Cooper by telling him "I'm going to call the cops and tell them an African American is threatening my life," A. Cooper did not play the victim card, she played the *other* race card.

In a chapter titled "Why am I always being told to 'check my privilege'?" from her book *So You Want to Talk About Race*, Oluo argues that, "The concept of privilege violates everything we've been told about fairness and everything we've been told about the American Dream of hard work paying off and good things happening to good people."[46] For those who openly wield white privilege the idea that there could be stoppages in the vectors through which it moves is not only unacceptable, it actually registers as violation. This is the *other* race card: A. Cooper was able to brazenly lie about the Black man standing in front of her—while recording her on his mobile phone, no less—because a powerful undercurrent of white privilege is the power of fiction. White privilege allows for the invention of whatever it wishes to believe or to make others believe in support of its position. The vectors that make white privilege possible can dissolve the blockages that impede its desires. When blockages appear it need only invent the terms required to remove the impediment or create conditions to discourage those who might interfere with its ostensible entitlements.

White privilege, when challenged, shows itself to be impervious to reproachment through sleights of hand used to weave its invented realities; its magical ability to morph its bearer into the victim of any given situation, and its inexhaustible capacity to counter claims of grievance with grievance claims of its own, no matter the depths of absurdity hazarded to achieve the necessary switcheroo; and then the stunning hypocrisies it nakedly wades into as it arms its bearers with a sense of fearlessness so that these same hypocrisies shape-shift for them from fiction into truth. Mists of possibility form around white privilege when it utilizes fiction as the basis for reality claims or when it attempts to root mendacity into solid ground. In sum, white privilege is the complete and utter absence of impediment across physical boundaries and psychic barriers.[47]

Colorblindness

One of the prevailing outgrowths of white privilege is colorblindness. It implies that one is incapable of seeing color, but the term refers more precisely to a conscious, willful *refusal* to see color. This refusal marks the threshold of post-racial logics. Take the idea that America had seemingly, as if by dint of magic, become a post-racial society overnight with the election of a Black president following Barack Obama's victory in 2008 and in the years leading up to his reelection in 2012. Obama's rise seemed to officially, if not definitively, authorize white America's longstanding desire to turn a blind eye to its racist past as many wondered aloud, how could racism exist with a Black president in office? But long before Obama's political ascent the notion that race was no longer worth figuring into the calculus of social and political decision-making operated under the guise of colorblindness.

Colorblind ideology emerged out of postwar discourses on racial liberalism. Its purported intent was to prop up equal opportunity legislation and anti-discrimination laws ostensibly designed to eliminate racial segregation. In reality, colorblind ideology was a mirage that appeared from a distance to support ameliorative provisions toward racial equality, but on closer inspection, were actually "premised centrally on strategic erasures within which the white norm and silent operations of white privilege do not disappear but, rather, become submerged within racial consciousness."[48]

Colorblindness serves two functions within both contemporary neoliberal and neoconservative contexts. On one hand, claiming colorblindness acts as a certificate of racial progressivism that signifies the ostensible embrace of counter-racist politics and social practices. When one claims they are colorblind it means to express in shorthand that not only are they not racist, but they are incapable of being racially biased, for how could one possibly discriminate on the grounds of color if they cannot see color? On the other hand, colorblindness functions as a smokescreen strategically deployed by hegemonic white power structures wishing to proffer the fiction that when we all embrace the proverbial melting pot of America and its ur-myth of rugged individualism, opportunity is open, accessible, and equally available to all. Take as an example the words of Dennis

Rice, a member of the Academy of Motion Pictures Arts and Sciences public relations branch, who in response to the #OscarsSoWhite movement declared, "I think we have to create an environment that supports diversity within our industry, but I'm color- and gender-blind when it comes to recognizing our art. You should look purely and objectively at the artistic accomplishment."[49] This, in essence, is the illusory blueprint of a meritocratic racist worldview, one that stands out boldly among the many profiles in sophistry around racial equality in Hollywood. To insist that one supports diversity and champions conditions of inclusion and in the same breath proclaim "colorblindness" is a rather stunning bit of rhetorical sleight of hand. Also cause for arrest is the suggestion that it is possible to adjudicate the "objective" merits of a film (or any work of art) as an accomplishment somehow shorn of its social or historical context. As Taylor sums it up, "Colorblindness and 'postracial' politics are vested in false ideas that the United States is a meritocratic society where hard work makes the difference between those who are successful and those who are not."[50] What, exactly, does it mean to not see color in a country that has, since its inception, been divided along a "color line?"

To say that one does not see color is, of course, to admit right away that one does in fact *see* color. In claims of colorblindness, we can immediately recognize at a rhetorical level that the assertion being made is, *I see color, but I elect to negate it*. Little further drilling down is needed to locate the deception at the center of colorblind ideology: by negating your color, I negate you and in place of you install a racially neutral object of my own invention. As Gloria Ladson-Billings observes, "Colorblindness is the way whites have always lived their lives, except when non-whites have advocated for similar opportunities, or privileges. Proponents of colorblindness believe that Blacks, Latinos and other people of color have not taken advantage of the opportunities the government so generously 'gave them', thus their inability to progress represents their own individual failure."[51]

Colorblindness proffers a fiction of racial neutrality while being "blind" to the ways that it induces a powerful amplifying effect in Black consciousness; in fact, colorblindness names precisely the internalization and intensification of racialized perception in Black consciousness. Ironically, colorblind ideology does not reduce Black racial anxiety under white supremacy, it amplifies racial anxiety in its disavowal of the material realities of Blackness. As color "vanishes" from the visual field of whiteness in statements like "I don't see color," the Black body is made crushingly aware of its own weight and presence in the world as Other.

Here we can locate a key dialectical relation between the "colorblind" look and the Black body, which brings about a distortion in the visual field called the *gaze*. In his description of Jacques Lacan's conception of the gaze in his book *Capitalism and Desire: The Psychic Cost of Free Markets*, Todd McGowan writes,

> The gaze exposes the tendentious nature of the apparently neutral visual field: what seems to be simply there to be seen becomes evident as a structure created around the subject's desire … In this sense, the trauma of encountering the gaze is nothing but the trauma of encountering the constitutive power of one's own desire in shaping what one sees even before one sees it.[52]

Through McGowan's account of the Lacanian gaze what we discover about colorblindness is that it brings about a distortion in the visual field in its desire to evacuate Blackness as difference even before Blackness appears (the "blind" in colorblind). The subject's desire to whitewash the visual field is ruptured by the Black body that refuses neutralization. What is revealed in this refusal is the structure of desire and its power to deform what it sees, and we discover that a neutral field of vision is impossible. This deformation of the seemingly neutral visual field is the gaze and in colorblindness, the gaze is writ large.

White Gaze

How we register racial difference in the visible world is bound up with complicated sets of forces informing our perception and understanding of the things we see, how our relationship to particular institutional powers and social allegiances guide these perceptions, and how we understand our own appearance as a thing caught within the visual field of the Other. This structure of appearance falls within the domain of the gaze. When the gaze becomes attached to whiteness it produces a specific set of conditions that reinforce formations of white supremacy and superiority.

The concept of the gaze holds considerable import in art history, film studies, continental philosophy, and critical theory. In each of these disciplines the gaze names a reciprocal exchange that marks a moment of recognizing and recognition, of appearing and appearance, of seeing and being seen, of addressing and being addressed. This sense of reciprocity reverberates widely through conceptions of the gaze in the twentieth and twenty-first centuries and develops particularly out of French intellectual traditions that have influenced much of the critical theory produced in the last century across the humanities. Jean-Paul Sartre has famously argued that consciousness of the self as subject is produced in and through encounters with the gaze of the Other (a foundational claim in Existentialism, a branch of continental philosophy for which he is often regarded as its progenitor). In these encounters, claims Sartre, we recognize that we are not only subjects in the world who perceive things around us, we also perceive ourselves as objects in the gaze of the Other and that recognition radically destabilizes our conceptions of coherency and freedom.[53] For Michel Foucault, the problem of subjective freedom in the gaze is bound up with systems of power and control in institutional apparatuses. In his analysis of the modern penal system, Foucault develops a theory of the panopticon that insists seeing oneself being seen was not necessary to maintain law and order. Rather, merely the inference of surveillance proved enough to control populations and compel adherence to law and legal order. In other words, the gaze and the power it implies need not be attached to a subject because its true power lies not in the visual field of the seer, but at the point when it becomes embodied by the seen. It is through this process of internalization that the gaze emerges.

For scholars of race and representation the gaze is bound up in the logics of oppression, but it also holds forth the possibility of challenge and opposition. In *Black Looks*, bell hooks notes that "The 'gaze' has been and is a site of resistance for colonized black people globally. Subordinates in relations of power learn experientially that there is a critical gaze, one that 'looks' to document, one that is oppositional."[54] Here hooks draws attention to the reciprocal structure of the gaze and the ways in which it allows Black people to experience the feeling of seeing themselves being seen, but with a crucial difference. For Black people it is not just that they see themselves being seen, but that they see themselves being seen *seeing*. This added layer of looking has proven to be a dangerous and threatening moment of recognition for Black people caught within a universal, all-encompassing white gaze. Black looks and the self-conscious recognition that Black looking is often not welcome and can, in many cases, lead to personal harm or injury has historically displaced and devalued Black positionality in a white ocularcentric world. For hooks, an oppositional gaze affords possibilities beyond representation or identification by altering the specular landscape for Black looking itself. hooks summarizes this idea when echoing the sentiment "Not only will I stare, I want my look to change reality."[55] As David Marriott notes in his reflections on Black men, "it is a question of who is looking and who is being looked at, a question which has always been central to the violence enacted by whites against black men."[56]

In what is certainly the most influential account of being caught within the distortional power of the white gaze, Frantz Fanon describes the feeling as an "unusual weight" that descends upon Black people and disrupts their relation to their own bodily integrity. In "The Lived Experience of the Black Man," Fanon recounts an incident in which a boy points at him and remarks to his mother, "Look, a Negro!" Fanon reports feeling "responsible not only for my body but for my race and ancestors. I cast an objective gaze over myself, discovered my Blackness my ethnic features; deafened by cannibalism, backwardness, fetishism, racial stigmas, slave traders ... ."[57] He describes the look of the boy and its discursive reinforcement (Look, a Negro!) as a white gaze. "In the colonial situation," writes Fanon, "the gaze of the other occupies the mind of the colonized, so that one does not have to experience a real encounter to feel the effects of the colonial gaze." He continues, "The white gaze, the only valid one, is dissecting me. I am *fixed*."[58] Fanon insists that in this reciprocal exchange, "My body is returned to me spread-eagled, disjointed, redone, draped in mourning ... ."[59]

I want to point out here some of the ways in which queries into the essence of Black existence crisscross over species claims and the very substance of Black being. David Marriott reads in this scene of Fanon's encounter with the French white boy that "Necessarily strangers to ourselves, *we have* to misunderstand ourselves, estranged from our selves and from each other. For we are *not s*omething smeared. The little French boy's combined fear and anxiety stain Fanon, mark him indelibly both within and without."[60] Returning to Fanon, he concludes finally, "I sense, I see in this white gaze that it's the arrival not of a new man, but of a new type of man, a new species. A Negro."[61] Here we see the persistence of an issue that has animated much discussion in critical race theory and a moment that returns us to the significance of ontology in studies of Black life, and which dovetails with the NBA players using their jerseys as a platform for resistance to assert the claim "I am a Man."

The white gaze holds the power to manipulate reality; it is a force of ontological rupture. It can mold myth into reality, like a ghost movie where an apparition is conjured and materializes in the visual field through an indescribable power. In the vector of the white gaze wallets transform into weapons, a bag of skittles and a hoodie pose a threat, a cell phone becomes a Glock 9mm handgun, toys become serrated blades. The distortional power of the white gaze is potent even when there are no objects to be deemed threatening. It can conjure panic from the imaginary into the real. To be Black and caught within the white gaze is like stepping in front of a funhouse mirror where what you are and know yourself to be becomes distorted beyond recognition.

The white gaze does not merely denote a perceptual field of racialization from a white perspective, it also marks the experience of being caught within the field of white *looking*, of having to bear the white gaze and to be interpellated by it as a racialized other. In other words, part of what is entailed by being addressed by a white gaze is to have to embody all of the suspicions, stereotypes, and prejudices that constitute its worldview. The white gaze is a vector of power; it is world making and world destroying. Like acid, it desubstantializes and breaks apart the forms of difference it comes into contact with. As Yancy observes, "In the end it's not about what the black body does, but what the white gaze sees."[62]

The Black Body

"Black bodies," writes Yancy, "continue to be marked, ontologically, as problem bodies and how the white gaze continues to mark those bodies through processes of interpellation (or hailing), power, denial, hegemony, and privilege even as so many white people believe that they are innocent of racism."[63] The Black body and the many forms of degradation, humiliation, and dehumanization thrust upon it over centuries of structural oppression are linchpin to the work of critical race theorists. In fact, it would be difficult for one to find a work of critical race theory that did not address in some substantive way the burdened and besieged histories of living life in Black bodies. There is voluminous discussion and debate on Black corporeality dating back to early scientific discourse and philosophy of the eighteenth century around race. These discussions were often supported by spurious systems of classification put in place to establish hierarchies between Europeans and the rest of the world's known inhabitants in order to justify colonial expansion and enterprise by way of indentured servitude. The terrain of the Black body and the quasi-scientific study of its musculature, epidermal makeup, and skeletal structure through the nineteenth and early twentieth centuries were used to support hypotheses that Blacks had more in common with animals and Neanderthals than human beings.[64] Though later debunked, these early "scientific" findings on Blackness and the assumptions around the hyper-sexuality and animalism of the Black body have persisted and continued to operate as twin poles of fear and fantasy in the white imaginary.

If we remain within the phenomenological coordinates of the white gaze, two crucial dimensions of the Black body as a discursive figure for identifying and redressing white supremacy's dominion over Black life come into view: how whiteness sees Black bodies, and how Black bodies internalize being seen by white looks. On this matter, Yancy is keen to point out that "The history of the Black body in North America is fundamentally linked to the history of whiteness, primarily as whiteness is expressed in the form of fear, sadism, hatred, brutality, terror, avoidance, desire, denial, solipsism, madness, policing, politics, and the production and projection of white fantasies."[65] While it is true that each of the terms Yancy offers to describe how whiteness sees Black bodies is indeed applicable, it is important that we put a finer point on the matter. These terms are not mutually exclusive nor independent of each other. To accept them as such is to come up directly against a set of contradictions that would have to reconcile how whiteness can fear, hate, and wish to avoid something that it equally or even more forcefully desires. This is the paradox at the center of white perceptions of Blackness and Black bodies. What we discover on closer inspection is that at the intersection of the white gaze and the Black body is a continual toggle between opposing affects: where there is fear there is also a want for intimacy, where there is repulsion there is also attraction, where there is disgust, there is envy, and where there is hatred, there is also desire.

The Black body has played two decisive roles in the field of the white gaze: it has been made into an object-thing, devoid of feeling and humanity, or capacities for thinking and reason; a commodity to be monetized, traded, sold, bartered, stockpiled, and eventually disposed of and replaced. On the other hand, the Black body has also functioned as a kind of screen on which is projected the erotic and sadistic fantasies of a white imaginary that essentializes Blackness as hyper-sexualized, possessing indefatigable and inordinate strength, lacking capacity for feeling, or whose threshold for bearing brutality and whose tolerance of pain and injury is so great as to make consideration of its consequences negligible. Ultimately, and in a strange inversion, it is the wish to possess and inhabit the very fantasy it has invented and mapped to a body it so despises.

In chattel slavery, the Black body was understood to be expendable (which is to say, fungible) even prior to birth. As Dorothy Roberts points out, the fetus in a Black mother's womb was a site of legal debate and contestation over property rights and ownership by the slave master, which in turn bracketed away kinship claims or considerations of biological attachment between Black parents and their progeny. Even at the level of reproduction the Black body was dehumanized and reduced, at best, to the trade of livestock.[66] Orlando Patterson uses the term "natal alienation" which on the one hand explicitly describes the traumatic separation Roberts recounts between mother and fetus (and later, child), but in a broader sense also describes Black bodies as "human proprietary objects" rather than simply "slaves" through one of the more psychologically devastating consequences of chattel slavery, and in a structure of psychic disenfranchisement that continues to resonate in the present. Natal alienation names a temporal disconnection from ancestry and any possibility of "anchoring the living present to any conscious community of memory."[67] It logically follows that being alienated from the past is to also have foreclosed the belief that one can intervene on the present to invent a possible future. As Patterson sums it up, "the fact of its possibility was experienced as an ever-present sense of impending doom that shadowed everything, every thought, every moment of ... existence."[68]

Saidiya Hartman also links the elasticity of Blackness and its fantasmatic configurations in the white imaginary to the fungibility of the commodity. In her landmark book *Scenes of Subjection: Terror, Slavery, and Unmaking in Nineteenth Century America*, Hartman reiterates the fundamental link between the pleasures and enjoyment chattel slavery afforded white slave owners and both the literal and figurative possession of the Black body when she writes,

> The fungibility of the commodity, specifically its abstractness and immateriality, enabled the black body or blackface mask to serve as the vehicle for white self-exploration, renunciation, and enjoyment ... since enjoyment is virtually unimaginable without recourse to the black body and the subjection of the captive, the diversions engendered by the dispossession of the enslaved, or the fantasies launched by the myriad uses of the black body.[69]

Woke

The origin of the term "woke" can be traced back to an article published in *The New York Times* on May 20, 1962, written by William Melvin Kelley titled "If You're Woke You Dig It."[70] In the piece, Kelley describes how colloquial words and phrases in mainstream culture (words like *cool*, *cat*, *chick*, and *dig*) originate out of Black vernacular before they are absorbed into everyday language. Though the term *woke* appears in the title, and while Kelley never refers to it again in the body of his essay, he does examine the influence and pervasiveness of what he calls "Negro idiom." Kelley observes that slang of his time is widely attributed to beatnik subculture, but that it is in fact "borrowed language" from Black people. In response to these acts of appropriation, Kelley argues, Black people "will consciously invent a new term as soon as they hear the existing one coming off of a white's lips."[71] The title of Kelley's piece appears to support this statement as he uses the term "woke" as a play on the term "dig," a word he notes most Americans know means "to understand" and had, by the 1960s, become common in the American lexicon.

Woke does not appear in slang usage again until 2008 when Georgia Anne Muldrow's song "Master Teacher" was rewritten and performed by Erykah Badu on her album *New Amerykah, Pt. 1 (World War 4)* on which she repeats the phrase "I stay woke." As Muldrow explains, when she began using the term "woke," she was describing her physical and spiritual exhaustion and her actual battle with sleep deprivation. But the phrase also connotes Black vigilance in the face of white oppression, cultural parasitism, and social injustice. Muldrow offers an analogy that not only clarifies the meaning of woke, but also bears striking resemblance to the narrative of *Get Out*:

> Woke is definitely a black experience—woke is if someone put a burlap sack on your head, knocked you out and put you in a new location and then you come to and understand where you are ain't home and the people around you ain't your neighbors. They're not acting in a neighborly fashion, they're the ones who conked you on your head. You got kidnapped here and then you got punked out of your own language, everything.[72]

In an August 8, 2012, tweet in support of Russian punk-rock band Pussy Riot, Badu would again use the phrase "stay woke" in response to their political persecution and legal prosecution on charges of "hooliganism" after a controversial performance in Moscow's Christ the Savior cathedral. In her tweet, Badu writes, "Truth requires no belief. Stay woke. Watch closely." In the years that followed, "stay woke" was used to refer to social and political awareness in the Black community, particularly in relation to the growing influence of the #blacklivesmatter movement. In the 2016 track, "Redbone" by Childish Gambino (heard in *Get Out*'s opening credit sequence), "stay woke" is used as a stern warning in the song's refrain:

> But stay woke
> Niggas creepin'
> They gon' find you
> Gon' catch you sleepin' (oh)
> Now stay woke
> Niggas creepin'
> Now don't you close your eyes

Gambino's use of "woke" aligns with Muldrow's usage when describing her physical exhaustion and the ongoing depletion of her energies as an artist and activist, while also playing off the sense implied that one should remain guarded and aware.

From the mid-2010s to the present, woke has incrementally lost its racialized focus on Black experience and has increasingly morphed into a liberal catchall naming any form of progressive action. In an article for *The New York Times*, titled "In Defense of Wokeness," Damon Young writes, "You were woke if you recycled, or maybe just retweeted an infographic on the virtues of recycling. White people were deemed woke. Some, painfully, even took it upon themselves to be the arbiters of wokeness."[73] Once the meaning-radius of woke expanded beyond the perimeter of Black experience and began saturating the mainstream lexicon, the term reached a point where it "described a racial awareness and cynicism so extra that it bordered on parody; where you're so awake that your 'third eye' saw things that aren't there." In the same article, Young also observes,

> It was no coincidence that this happened alongside Barack Obama's political ascent. Being liberal—and communicating exactly how radical you wanted people to believe you were— had cultural benefits… ."I would have voted for Obama for a third term if I could" wasn't just the most effective joke in the movie "Get Out." It was the bumper sticker real-life (white) progressives stuck to their foreheads.[74]

Woke is a derivative of wake. To wake is to regain consciousness after sleep or to be roused from sleep back to consciousness. Wake can also mean to bring awareness to or become alert and stir into an active or conscious state. Woke idiomatically plays off these various definitions of wake, but there are other senses of the term *wake* that have been powerfully deployed in recent critical race theory as a way of attending to the past traumas of transatlantic slavery and how they continue to resonate through Black America Now.

Wake

Christina Sharpe's *In the Wake: On Blackness and Being* develops the term "wake" as a framework for understanding how anti-Blackness borne out of transatlantic slavery con- tinues to haunt Black life in the present. Borrowing a turn of phrase from William Faulkner who famously wrote "The past is not dead. It is not even past," Sharpe navigates Black America Now using "wake" and its whole range of meanings as a theoretical compass. Some of the meanings Sharpe evokes include "wake" as consciousness or a state of wakefulness; wakes as tracks left on a body of water's surface by a ship, or the disturbance left by a body moving in water; wakes as agitated flows in the air currents behind a vessel or object in flight; a "wake" can also refer to holding vigil in the presence of the dead before burial.

"Wake," for Sharpe, serves as a metaphor that crystallizes a central premise of contemporary critical race theory eloquently articulated by Hartman who writes,

> If slavery persists as an issue in the political life of black America, it is not because of an antiquarian obsession with bygone days or the burden of a too-long memory, but because black lives are still imperiled and devalued by a racial calculus and a political arithmetic that were entrenched centuries ago. *This is the afterlife of slavery—* skewed life chances, limited access to health and education, premature death, incarceration, and impoverishment, I, too, am the afterlife of slavery.[75]

Following Hartman, Sharpe affirms the persistence of slavery as an issue for Black life in America not as a distant epoch that stubbornly remains a point of fixity separate from the present. Instead, she insists that slavery has produced a wake that has swept up Black life in its still rippling aftermath. Wakes are "processes" that allow us to think about our relations to the dead and to a past that is not past. These processes make legible the innumerable ways in which Black people have been living and continue to live in the afterlife of slavery. This is what Sharpe calls "living in the wake."

So what does it mean to be Black and to be living in the wake? Like the diminution of Black life Roberts describes, or the concept of social death and "natal alienation" elaborated by Patterson, living in the wake is living in a state of propertied existence in perpetuity where Black non/Being and non/ status is ontological. To live in the wake is to live everyday through the terrible historical arc of slavery from antebellum to the present: "living the historically and geographically dis/ continuous but always present and endlessly reinvigorated brutality in, and on, our bodies while even as that terror is visited on our bodies the realities of that terror are erased."[76]

Thus, to be in and of the wake names a full and complete immersion in forms of terror not merely enacted on and against Black bodies, but constitutive of Black life itself and made visible through the continued policies of stop and frisk, the wildly disproportionate incarceration of Black men, and the pervasive atmosphere of Black death and vulnerability as the ground of American democracy. In an observation that aligns her scholarly program with the tenets of Afropessimism, Sharpe asks, "What will happen then if instead of demanding justice we recognize (or at least consider) that the very notion of justice ... produces and requires Black exclusion and death as normative?"[77]

In fusing separate definitions of "wake" ("Wake" as consciousness and "wake" as disturbance), Sharpe proposes a compelling alternative to pursuing social justice remedies within the structural coordinates of the very forces producing and enforcing the conditions of abjection that need rectifying. Living in the wake incites the possibility of Black being as a form of *consciousness* that countervails social and political pursuits for justice and resolution.[78] To embody this countervailing consciousness in the wake "is to occupy and be occupied by the continuous and changing present of slavery's as yet unresolved unfolding."[79] Another way of expressing this dialectic of occupying and being occupied by slavery's aftermath in the present brings us back to the refrain of "Redbone" and its plea to Black listeners to "stay woke." But what Sharpe's notion of consciousness seems to call for is not that Black folk "stay woke," but that they "*be woke*."

This sense of *being* woke is what Sharpe calls "wake work." Wake work names modes of consciously wading into and inhabiting "quotidian disasters in order to ask what, if anything, survives this insistent Black exclusion, this ontological negation, and how do literature, performance, and visual culture observe and mediate this un/survival?"[80] This turn to Black expressive culture is crucial to the metaphorical power of the "wake" and to understanding "wake work" as an active, intentional form of being woke. Sharpe says she looks to Black artistic forms "that do not explain or resolve the question of this exclusion in terms of assimilation, inclusion, or civil and human rights, but rather depict aesthetically the impossibility of such resolutions by representing the paradoxes of Blackness within and after the legacies of slavery's denial of Black humanity."[81] In the context of these observations, Jordan Peele's *Get Out*, I will argue in the following chapter, is one of the great achievements of "wake work" in American narrative cinema.

Trans/plantation

If the afterlife of slavery haunts Black life in the present and the past that is not past keeps Black being submerged in its wake, it is necessary to come to terms with how the conditions of slavery continue to be reproduced in Black America Now. The subject of transatlantic slavery cannot be thought apart from a plantation system birthed from the marriage of terror and capitalism that motored colonial expansion beyond the perimeter of Europe. A plantation, as anthropologist Sidney W. Mintz explains, is "a politico-economic invention, a colonial frontier institution, combining non-European slaves and European managerial skill with territorial control of free and subtropical lands in the mass, mono-crop production of agricultural commodities for European markets."[82] Plantations, in their most basic sense, are but one feature of a broader capitalist enterprise structured around the violent seizure and extraction of Black bodies from their native lands, and the transportation of those Black bodies across the Atlantic to the New World where through the complete inversion of their humanity they are transformed from sentient beings into commodities, instruments of labor, and the assets of a slave owner.

Missing from Mintz's dutiful definition is the psychic wreckage of the slave's existence in the plantation system. The plantation marks a geographic location in physical space, but it also designates a perimeter in which natal alienation through geographies of Black dismantling and destitution is inaugurated. The plantation system then not only coincides with the "politico-economic" practice of transatlantic slavery, but, quite literally, it emerges when and only when Black bodies are installed in these geospatial zones of terror. Thus, a plantation is not merely a politico-economic invention, it is, above and beyond all, a site of possession. The plantation system is the explicit institution and economic leveraging of an immense power imbalance between master and slave, and the unilateral application of that power-over-life in every facet of the slave's propertied existence from labor extraction to ownership claims on the fetus in a Black woman's womb. If we are "in the wake" and continue to live the afterlives of slavery, how is plantation life and its logic reproduced in the present? What other forms of possession might a thriving (albeit clandestine) "plantation system" allow for in Black America Now?

To begin, we might consider Sharpe's use of the prefix "trans" as a mode for conceptualizing the conditions of contemporary Black life: "translation, transatlantic, transgression, trans-gender, transformation, transmogrification, transcontinental, transfixed, trans-Mediterranean, transubstantiation (by which process we might understand the making of bodies into flesh and then into fungible commodities while retaining the appearance of flesh and blood), transmigration, and more," all serve as ways of conceptualizing Black being by trying to get "at something *about* or *toward* the range of trans*formations enacted on and by Black bodies."[83] To this suggested *more*, I add the term *trans/plantation* (from the Latin "*trans*" meaning "on the other side of" or "to cross from one side to the other") as a concept addressing the perpetuation of plantation logic and the institutional structures of indentured servitude that operate clandestinely in the present. The seizure of Black bodies, and more abstractly the inner life world of Black being, for purposes of white profit and plenitude is not limited to the domain of physical capture. Under colorblind neoliberalism it aims more insidiously at capturing the Black body from *within*.

The common definitions of transplantation refer to the labor of moving or transferring an object or thing between locations, typically uprooting and replanting something from one place to another. Transplantation is also removing living tissue or an organ and implanting it in another part of the body or in another body entirely. I split *trans* from *plantation* in order to emphasize the separate but related experience of a corporeal and spatial crossing from one side to another and to evoke specifically the plantation as a site of annihilation through possession. To this end, I want first to clarify how *trans/plantation* differs from how "transplantation" is understood in the sense that critical race theorists like Sylvia Wynter use it when describing how slaves mitigated the feeling of natal alienation borne of the extractive violence committed against Black bodies through the Middle Passage.

Wynter argues that the experience of alienation is a dynamic event that alters the slave's relation to the world through an internalized awareness of that alienation. Such moments of recognition produce what Wynter calls *cultural metamorphosis*: the *replanting* of indigenous traditions and reimagined practices of Black creativity in the plantation system as a form of resistance to the slave owner's attempts at total dehumanization and ontological erasure.[84] In his book *Necropolitics*, Achille Mbembe offers an example of this act of "transplantation" when he writes, "Breaking with uprootedness and the pure world of things of which he is a mere fragment, the slave is able to demonstrate the protean capabilities of the human bond through music and the body itself that was supposedly possessed by another."[85] For Wynter, the integrity of the slave's inner life world is essential to this process of "transplanting" Black cultural roots in the soil of the New World as a way of domesticating the destructive, alien territory of the plantation. In the paradox of fusing *trans* to *plantation* by way of splitting, I mean to illuminate not a territorial crossing of Black bodies through geographic space from one location to another, or the relocating and re-rooting of cultural traditions in alien worlds as acts of resistance and survival, but rather to name a violational movement, specifically from white *into* Black, that seeks to dissolve the slave's inner life world to make way for whiteness. The cultural metamorphosis that Wynter argues for and the acts of resistance it makes possible as Mbembe describes them are thus actively negated by an eliminative process that *trans/plants* the corrosive conditions of plantation logic and the forms of desubjectification they inaugurate into both the physical and the psychic life of Black being.

I follow Sharpe here when she claims that "slavery trans* all desire as it made some people into things, some into buyers, sellers, owners, fuckers, and breeders of ... Black flesh."[86] Taking her cue from Dionne Brand who writes "That one door [the door of no return] transformed us into bodies empty of being, bodies emptied of self-interpretation, into which new interpretations could be placed," Sharpe designates the Middle Passage as an ontological rupture in the world of Black being ("the door of no return") that refracts its violence through a *trans*historical spectrum "whether *we* made *that* passage or not."[87] Contra Wynter, Sharpe's description of trans* in the context of slavery conveys a scene where the terrain of the plantation is a rupture *trans*forming Black people into "empty bodies" lacking the capacity for self-interpretation, allowing for new interpretations to be implanted. This transformation is ontological and in this diminishment of Black psychic integrity a clearing is made for worlds of white privilege to trans/plant a whole constellation of oppressive logics into the Black body.

Trans/plantation names processes by which the psychic integrity of Black personhood is assailed in magnitudes so great that any assurance of preserving subjectivity through acts of cultural bonding is utterly foreclosed. "Slave life, in many ways, is a form of death-in-life," writes Mbembe.[88] Where "transplantation" refers to acts of Black re-rooting, trans/plantation describes the uprooting and replanting of white substitutions *in* Blackness; it is a form of slave life (social death) where white oppressors not only possess the Black body materially, they enter into a substitutive relation with the Black body so as to possess it subjectively from *within*. What is distinctive about this *within* is that it does not refer to manipulation or control in a political or ideological sense; rather, it refers, quite literally, to a form of physical possession by way of dispossession where whiteness inhabits Blackness. Put another way, trans/plantation is possession by possession. It is a form of "haunted life," as David Marriott might call it, because it remains an extension of the plantation system, which relied heavily upon the replaceability of the Black body as a commodity to be bought, sold, owned, or bred. Here it is helpful to recall Hartman's observations (no doubt informed by Hegel) that "the fungibility of the commodity makes the captive body an abstract and empty vessel vulnerable to the projections of others' feelings, ideas, desires, and values; and, as property, the dispossessed body of the enslaved is the surrogate for the master's body since it guarantees his disembodied universality and acts as the sign of his power and dominion."[89] Hartman deftly articulates this crucial dimension to the experience of slavery as the captive Black body rendered commodity was *trans*formed into an empty vessel to better serve as a surrogate body for the master who, as owner of that body, was free to project (or better, *plant*) into his surrogate whatever aspects of himself, be it physical or fantasmatic, he wished.

In the following chapter, I show how *Get Out* envisions neo-slavery in Black America Now as a process of trans/plantation, but a brief overview of another influential Black horror film (one that Jordan Peele was recently involved in remaking, no less) will show that the twin poles of fear and fantasy and the forms of white substitution they engender have long been expressed as possession by possession.

Candyman and *Trans/plantation*

Bernard Rose's *Candyman* (1992) tells the story of Helen Lyle, a white graduate student in the Department of Anthropology at the University of Illinois, Chicago, whose dissertation research on urban legends leads her to pursue the myth of Candyman. According to legend, Candyman was the son of a freed slave who, though trained as a portraitist and integrated into "polite society" near the turn of the twentieth century, was brutally lynched after it was discovered he had fallen in love and impregnated the daughter of a wealthy white landowner. Candyman's painting hand was severed, his body smeared with honey from the combs of a nearby apiary, and stung to death by bees before his remains were burned on a pyre and his ashes scattered on grounds that would later become Chicago's Cabrini Green housing project. A vengeful spirit haunted by lost love in death, the specter of Candyman haunts back, appearing behind his would-be victims with a hook for a hand ready to eviscerate whosoever dares to speak his name five times into a mirror.

Helen learns from Black custodial workers at UCI that a woman named Ruthie Jean was recently murdered in a Cabrini Green high rise and word on the street is Candyman is the culprit. Helen and her Black research partner, Bernadette, decide to visit Cabrini Green to learn more about the connection between the crime, the legend of Candyman and why the residents of a housing project are attributing violence in their community to a Black phantom. Prior to her safari into "Candyman country," Helen discovers that the condominium she and her professor husband live in was constructed from the same blueprints as the buildings in Cabrini Green. This is a key detail since Helen is able to corroborate the claim that Ruthie Jean's killer came through her bathroom wall after discovering the mirror on the medicine cabinet of her own bathroom is removable allowing for easy access into the adjoining unit. When they arrive at the scene of the crime, just as Helen had suspected, she is able to open the bathroom mirror in Ruthie Jean's apartment and, as it were, go through the looking glass.

Suspending momentarily what Helen finds on the other side of the mirror it is worth noting the irony of how the film frames her and Bernadette's trespassing in other people's homes (as Ruthie Jean's neighbor Anne Marie tells them,

"You don't belong going through people's apartments and thangs") as cause for worry over *their* safety. In the economy of the narrative concern for the residents of the Cabrini Green housing complex is an afterthought, instead the film marshals concern for the white woman and her token Black tag along who, uninvited, enter a Black community in dogged pursuit of their ethno-anthropological curiosities. Much has already been written about the film's sophisticated critique of spatial segregation through urban planning initiatives and gentrification in Chicago's urban/suburban divide, particularly how white people come to occupy urban space when the perimeter of white middle class geographies needs expanding.[90] These discussions hardly require repeating here, but as it relates to what I am calling *trans/plantation*, I want to call attention to the ease and comfort with which Helen crosses over into Black spaces when it proves expedient to her professional (which is to say capitalist) advancement, and how spatial trespassing and uninvited crossings leveraging Black oppression tied to slavery—made possible by white privilege— eventually result in scenes of possession by possession.

This fact is made clear as we watch Helen navigate Ruthie Jean's apartment, climbing through the same holes in the walls as Ruthie Jean's killer had before her. Eventually, Helen approaches one of the holes with her camera in hand framed in a medium shot. As she begins taking pictures of the room through the hole, the camera zooms out and we discover, before Helen does, that spray-painted around the hole is an image of Candyman's face screaming. Leaving little to subtlety, not only is Helen trespassing a scene of Black death, but she also enters the space as if being expelled out of Candyman's body through his muted screams. In this richly symbolic image it is Helen who is already inside of Candyman before Candyman haunts Helen.

It is important to recall that "*trans*" means "on the other side of," or "to cross from one side to the other." As if white fantasy itself were hatching from its Black chrysalis, Helen's symbolic emergence from Candyman's body designates a transfer point between physical spaces, but it also marks the first moment in the film when the divide between Helen and Candyman begins to blur. The film makes clear that prior to the murders Helen will apparently commit, murders she will adamantly attribute to Candyman and his haunting her with seductive declarations ("Be my victim!"), it is she who first possesses the possessor; it is she who haunts the haunter.

There, captured in a single shot, is the scene of trans/plantation foreshadowing Helen's displacement of Candyman and her embodiment of the myth by supplanting her white body in place of his Black body and writing over his history with her own. In the film's closing moments, Helen leads Candyman to believe that she will "be his victim" in order to rescue Anne Marie's baby who is buried under scraps of wood and discarded furniture being used for a large bonfire. As the Cabrini Green residents set the kindling alight, Helen executes her deception and in true "white savior" form snatches the baby from Candyman and crawls from the fire to reunite Anne Marie with her little boy, burning to death along with Candyman in the process. In the end, Helen extends the logic of the plantation by exposing the fungibility at the core of the Candyman myth and reinscribes his postbellum lynching in the present by destroying and displacing him from the mythic status he had hoped to sustain through her love (which, in the end, is arguably little more than the narcissistic projections of Helen than a haunting, a mark of her own compulsive fascination and obsession with advancement vis-à-vis Blackness and the Black body) and, in her own death becomes the very myth she tried so diligently to debunk, rescuing one Black body from death while casting another back to death so that she might flourish as its replacement. As Eric Lott puts it, "This means Candyman the specter walks the line between white fetish and the afterlife of social death—the racist violence that originally killed him and its new variation as constituted by carceral postwar 'urban renewal' complexes such as Cabrini."[91]

It is not coincidental that Helen's cooptation of Black mythology in *Candyman* appears to be similar with *Get Out* and its own trans/plantationary logic.[92] Helen's embodiment (literal and figurative) of Candyman is not dissimilar to the kind of embodiment achieved through the coagula process where Black consciousness is displaced from its body so that white consciousness can possess it from within. Candyman does not just step through the door of no return, *he is the door of no return*, already fixed and emptied for Helen to freely crisscross identificatory thresholds and place new meanings—new "interpretations," as Brand calls it—into him.

The Final Brother

While the intuitive Black character is common in American horror films, the generic convention that most commonly determines protagonism and establishes paradigms of survival is what Carol Clover calls "the final girl." In her book *Men, Women and Chainsaws: Gender in the Modern Horror Film*, Clover argues these films inaugurate an archetypal shift where women who traditionally functioned as objects to be looked at or as victims in need of saving by a male protagonist undergo a role reversal. What Clover discovers is that a female protagonist—a "final girl"—tends not only to be the last survivor of the modern horror film, she is its guiding agential force in defeating and destroying the monster—or at least, temporarily suspending the monster's murderous impulses until the inevitable sequel.

There are several recurring characteristics that identify the "final girl" and distinguish her from others in her group: she tends to be morally centered, is often portrayed as virginal and avoids or shows restraint from partaking in illicit pleasures such as drugs and drinking (activities that mark others for death), proves to be preternaturally resourceful, is portrayed as having masculine qualities (name, dress, comportment ...), and is the one who ultimately destroys the monster or sets up the monster's elimination via institutional forces. According to Clover, the "final girl" signals a dramatic departure from the typically gendered divisions between heroes and victims in horror movies and the identificatory attachments formed between the genre's predominantly male audience and its male characters. She permits fluid forms of identification across gender lines, as male spectators can align their gaze with a female protagonist through her desexualization, physical strength, and her capacities for problem solving.

While Clover's concept of the final girl identifies an important trend that overturns fixed notions of survivability in the horror genre, there are some narrative elements that remain consistent despite this blurring of protagonist gender lines. All horror films are essentially narratives in which "normality is threatened by the Monster."[93] In horror films of the classical period the destruction of the monster and the restitution of "normality" are achieved, almost invariably, through the intervention of social institutions (police, church, military, medicine) whose primary focus is to preserve the safety and sanctity of the heterosexual monogamous couple and/or the nuclear family (or simply "normality," as it were). In the horror films of the modern period, "normality" and the monster are intertwined. The monster threatening "normality" is not a foreign entity or "Other," but comes from within the very "normality" being threatened: cops become maniac cops, doctors try to bridge the gap between life and death, priests lose their faith or court and conjure demonic spirits, brothers, mothers and fathers are all potential killers. The final girl emerges as dominant trope in the horror film at precisely the moment when the genre becomes, as Robin Wood puts it, deeply incoherent: the longstanding Hays Code rule that all monsters must die at the end of horror films is deregulated, institutional forces are no longer effective in stopping the monster, patriarchal figures are rendered useless or traitorous, and endings are left open-ended and unresolved. Though the modern period of the horror film is marked by a lack of resolution as the monsters in these films are rarely, if ever, decisively destroyed, going back to Wood's basic formula is crucial to an understanding of race in American horror films and what makes Chris Washington such a unique protagonist.

"Normality" in every sense of the word refers to worlds of white privilege, and the final girl is tasked not only with destroying the monster, but also coded in her survival is the very possibility that "normality" could and should be restored. This encoding of "normality" occurs in and through the final girl's whiteness. If we add a touch of specificity to Clover's formula, the final girl is almost invariably *the final white girl*. Some of the more notable examples of this character type include: Mari Collingwood (*The Last House on the Left*, 1972), Jess Bradford (*Black Christmas*, 1974), Sally Hardesty (*The Texas Chainsaw Massacre*, 1974), Laurie Strode (*Halloween*, 1978), Nancy Thompson (*A Nightmare on Elm Street*, 1984), and Sydney Prescott (*Scream*, 1996): all white women.

The monster's threat to "normality" presumes that there is a "normality" to be threatened. Conflicts between monster and institution (classical) or conflicts from within American institutions (modern) are, ultimately, all conflicts in which a protagonist seeks to restore "normality" and return to a world as it was prior to the monster's arrival. But what happens when there is no "normality" to begin with, or no "normality" to fight for or even attempt to restore? What happens if there is not a time *before* the monster's arrival? This is a radical conception of the horror film that destabilizes Wood's basic premise (a premise, it should be noted, that has served as the bedrock for horror scholarship for more than four decades).

One of the constitutive elements of narrative is that all sentient beings can experience redemption. But, as Wilderson points out, if "history and redemption are the weave of narrative, as provocative as it may sound, history and redemption (and therefore narrative itself) are inherently anti-Black."[94] It is worth repeating here Wilderson observation that "Blackness *is* social death, which is to say that there was never a prior moment of plenitude, never a moment of equilibrium, never a moment of social life."[95] This reading of the horror film's basic formula in the context of Blackness offers, I think, an effective framework for understanding the narrative of *Get Out*, its points of contact with and departure from other

American horror films before it, and the dilemmas facing Chris as the prototype of what I am calling here the *final brother*.

Using the character of Chris Washington, I want to offer a preliminary sketch of the *final brother* to illustrate how strikingly divergent (in fact, how completely inverted) the conditions of survivability are for a lone Black survivor and a lone white woman in a horror movie narrative. Below is a chart of basic oppositions:

The Final Girl	*The Final Brother*
–White woman	–Black man
–Signifies possibility of a return to "normality"	–Signifies impossibility of a return to "normality"
–Subject of the white gaze (conduit)	–Object of the white gaze (commodity)
–Cross-gender identification possible	–Cross-racial identification impossible
–Narrative (social) death optional	–Narrative (social) death integral
–Virginal	–Raped
–Uses intuition to survive	–Ignores intuition to sustain white comfort

In the following chapter, I track Chris' path through the story arc of *Get Out* as the prototype of the *final brother*. It is a character type that is by necessity more speculative than empirical, for unlike Clover, I do not have a cross-section of examples to map out a decades long tendency. But I want to suggest that the lack of examples from which to draw comparisons is not a shortcoming, but rather signals its importance and underscores the urgency to develop a working model. While it is true that seeing a morally centered, vice-avoiding, white virginal heroine survive a horror film narrative proved to be a significant development in the genre from the early-1970s and beyond, to see a lone Black protagonist who survives the Monster/Master and tries to restore "normality," even today, is a sight that is nothing short of astonishing. In other words, because there are few (if any) films with which to compare and thus chart patterns of development for lone Black survivors, using the paradigm of the final girl as a framework for conceptualizing Black protagonism in the horror genre opens up new and productive areas of inquiry. It is at this juncture where contemporary critical race theory and studies of Blackness in the horror film meet that the *final brother* emerges as a trope of its own.

CHAPTER TWO

Critical Race Theory and Jordan Peele's *Get Out*

At the bottom of our news tonight there's been a new animal aimed in the direction of falling off the face of the earth. Yes, young black teenagers are reported to be the oldest, and the newest, animals added to the endangered species list. As of now the government has not made steps to preserve the Blacks. When asked why a top government official adds, "Because they make good game."

—Ice Cube, "Endangered Species," *AmeriKKKa's Most Wanted*

This mock news sketch is an interlude from Ice Cube's 1990 debut studio album *AmeriKKKa's Most Wanted*; however, it could just as readily have come from the world of Jordan Peele's *Get Out*. In the sketch a news broadcaster describes young Black people as a precarious population poised to fall "off the face of the earth," animals whose dwindling numbers have resulted in being added to the endangered species list (a dubious distinction assigned to a species facing extinction). The twist, of course, is that when asked if the government plans to intervene in the dereliction of Black life rather than pivoting to the standard political rhetoric of prefabricated untruths, the government official being questioned instead candidly admits that because young Black people "make good game" their expendability must be secured; in other words, it is not Black life that needs preserving, but its expendability that should be guarded and maintained. The admission that young Black people "make good game" (a phrase we can take to mean capture, elimination, and tokening) vivifies the social death of Blackness and corroborates the tensions raised on the status of Black life in Afropessimism when Wilderson insists that: " ... the mind would have to see a person with a heritage of rights and claims, whose rights and claims are being violated. This is not the way Slaves, Blacks, function in the collective unconscious."[1]

Nearly three decades separate the release of *AmeriKKKa's Most Wanted* and *Get Out*, and yet this image of dehumanized Black life reduced to little more than prey or sport in the machinery of white supremacy, or otherwise retaining its violable status in worlds of white privilege persists. Critical race theory on its own does not account for how aesthetic practices raise questions of race or interrogate how its social, political, and cultural dimensions are represented. However, when utilized as an analytical tool for probing race and representation it puts performative examples of institutionalized anti-Blackness into context, throws light on how and why Blackness appears and reappears in specific aesthetic forms, and makes available critical frameworks for examining transgenerational legacies of racial violence.

This chapter applies critical race theory as a methodology for film analysis. It provides a close reading of *Get Out* drawing on each of the key terms in the previous chapter and their related concepts to perform a race reading of the film. By bringing some of the pressing questions around race in the cultural climate of Black America Now to bear on a film that has proven critically and financially successful despite its themes of racial antagonism, the questions that come immediately into the foreground pertain to the film's reception.

Genre Trouble

In mid-November of 2017, the Hollywood Foreign Press announced the nomination of *Get Out* for a Golden Globe Award in the category of "Best Musical or Comedy." The nomination sparked considerable controversy across social media. Much of the backlash centered around the notion that a largely non-Black voting body showed itself incapable of taking seriously the film's depictions of white liberal racism, the abduction, purchase, and enslavement of Black bodies, the structural perpetuation of Black indentured servitude for profit, and the overt fantasies and fetishizations it mobilizes in the white imaginary. Lil Rel Howery (the actor who plays Rod in the film) addressed the controversy on Twitter with a post that read: "But if I can be honest this is weird to me … There is nothing funny about racism … Was it that unrealistic lol." Jordan Peele, also responding to the matter on Twitter with acuity added, "*Get Out* is a documentary."

If there was a single point around which outrage coalesced it was the perceived insensitivity to the Black community that a story unambiguously about white supremacy and the clandestine forms it takes under neoliberalism would be deemed a comedy by a longstanding institution like the Hollywood Foreign Press. As Peele observed, "The reason for the visceral response to this movie being called a comedy is that we are still living in a time in which African American cries for justice aren't being taken seriously. It's important to acknowledge that though there are funny moments, the systemic racism that the movie is about is very real."[2] The Hollywood Foreign Press has a history of nominating films in categories that seem questionable or erroneous, but I would submit that the film's categorical misplacement and the indeterminacy around its classification have less to do with the structure or narrative of the film, its "funny moments" as Peele describes, or the question of how best to situate it within available generic categories, and has more to do with the signifying power of Blackness. Put differently, it is Black protagonism that destabilizes the generic legibility of the film as "horror" and produces this indeterminacy.

Much of this confusion can be attributed to how representations of Blackness in Hollywood have historically fused the genres of comedy and horror. It is telling that apart from *Get Out*, the most successful Black cast/Black made horror films have all been parodies of the genre, chief among them the *Scary Movie* franchise developed by The Wayans Brothers (of *In Living Color* fame) spanning 2000–13. These films draw on both stereotypical portrayals of Black characters in horror movies and, more broadly, on racist perceptions of Black people in America for much of its humor. For example, in *Scary Movie* (2000) a white teenage girl named Drew is killed at a high school and several news channels arrive to report live from the scene. The camera pans across several reporters standing next to their vans delivering the news with poise and professionalism before stopping on a reporter from "Black TV." Already sitting in the passenger side of the news van, the Black reporter anxiously declares, "Reporting live for Black TV, white folks are dead and we're getting the fuck outta here!" The van speeds away with its panicked Black passengers before the doors can close. The scene continues with three women discussing the possibility of being interviewed on TV when the Black women among them says, "The Press only wants to interview the most ignorant person they can find." Cut to Shorty (Marlon Wayans), an overzealous Black teenager being interviewed by reporters: "I'm on TV! Oh shit, first Cops and now this?! Imma be a star, son!" The reporter asks, "What would have been your last words to Drew?" to which Shorty unsurprisingly replies, "Run, bitch! Run!"

In *Scary Movie 3* (2003), Brenda (a Black woman) watches the cursed video made famous in *The Ring* franchise (2002–17) before calling out to her white friend in another room: "Cindy, the news is on. Another little white girl done fell down a well. Fifty black people get they ass beat by police today, but the whole world gotta stop for one little whitey damn hoe." In Ezio Greggio's *The Silence of the Hams* (1994), a precursor to the horror parody boom of the 2000s, the beating of Rodney King by the Los Angeles Police Department is mockingly restaged replete with King's infamous plea, "Can't we all just get along?" The humor in these scenes hinges on a reality principle. That a Black woman would see an iconic scene from a horror film and mistake it for the news, or that one of the few appearances of Black people in an early horror parody would mock amateur video of the Rodney King beating widely circulated on broadcast news supports Peele's quip that "*Get Out* is a documentary."

In the many interviews Peele gave following the film's release the question of categorical placement remained an area of contention. While he has steadfastly aligned *Get Out* with the horror genre and has gone into great detail citing the horror films that influenced the film's plot design and visual language, Peele has also acknowledged the limitations that any single genre affords a text as a categorical marker or as a framework that monolithically determines its meaning. In an interview published in *New York* magazine's Vulture section, Peele admits to not knowing which genre best suits *Get Out*: "I was trying to figure out what genre this movie was, and horror didn't quite do it. Psychological thriller didn't do it." His solution to the problem was to develop a category he calls the "social thriller." In the social thriller, Peele tells us, "The bad guy is society—these things that are innate in all of us, and provide good things, but ultimately prove that humans are always going to be barbaric, to an extent."[3] In the introduction to the edited volume *Jordan Peele's Get Out: Political Horror*, Dawn Keetley adds a finer point to Peele's description when she writes, "The distinctive terrain of the 'social thriller' is that its monster is intractably human, the 'demon' inextricably part of the very real fabric of society."[4] Useful as these definitions of the "social thriller" may be, they raise questions as to the need for an entirely new paradigm or why available generic categories do not appear to adequately describe *Get Out*. If we understand the "social" in "social thriller" in the sense Peele suggests, then "social" refers to society itself as an irreducibly imperiling force that will inevitably manifest its innermost potential for cruelties upon persons within a given community. But is this not, already partially, a definition of the modern horror film? I concluded the previous chapter by noting the importance of Robin Wood's contributions to horror film studies and a closer look at his work provides some needed clarification on the role of society in the genre.

In his groundbreaking essay "An Introduction to the American Horror Film," Wood persuasively argues that all horror films express societal fears through culturally specific forms of repression. The locus of cultural repression in American society, Wood tells us, is sexuality. Closely linked to the repression of sexuality is the concept of the Other, "which bourgeois ideology cannot recognize or accept but must deal with in one of two ways: either by rejecting and if possible annihilating it, or by rendering it safe and assimilating it, converting it as far as possible into a replica of itself."[5] Repression and otherness in the American horror film come together precisely in the domain of the social. This fact is made apparent in the eight examples Wood claims are characteristic of otherness and repression in the genre:

1   Other people
2   Women
3   The proletariat
4   Other cultures
5   Ethnic groups within the culture
6   Alternative ideologies or political systems
7   Deviations from ideological sexual norms
8   Children

Alone or taken together, the "fabric of American society" is woven from these threads and the many iterations of monstrosity in modern American horror films are all products, in one form or another, of society. Therefore, to suggest that the conflation of monstrosity and the social is the distinct terrain of the "social thriller" is to ignore the intervention Wood's landmark essay makes and its widespread influence on the field of horror studies.

To more emphatically make the point we can look to filmmakers, critics, and historians of the American horror film who generally share in Wood's conviction that Alfred Hitchcock's 1960 *Psycho* marks a turning point in the evolution of the horror film. Wood claims, "Since *Psycho*, the Hollywood cinema has implicitly recognized Horror as both American and familial."[6] This development dramatically departs from the genre's earlier preoccupations with foreign and outside threats that had dominated horror films throughout the first half of the twentieth century. Prior to 1960, American institutions were seen as the solution to defeating the monster and restoring "normality," but—following Wood—critic Marc Jancovich points out, "the film identifies the American nuclear family as the source of the threat ... *Psycho* is therefore a critique of the institution which [Wood] sees as fundamental to American society, the patriarchal family."[7]

Cultural Studies scholar Paul Wells has also summarized Hitchcock's contribution to the horror genre by insisting that *Psycho* first posited the idea of the modern monster as mutable, protean, unspeakable, unknowable, but also frighteningly domesticated. Wells argues that before *Psycho* cultural institutions in horror films could be relied upon to offer closure and security, but:

> *Psycho* sought to challenge this perspective by directly implicating the viewer in an amoral universe grounded in the psychic imperatives of its protagonists ... [it] essentially defines the parameters of the text and sub-text of the genre as a whole. It is the moment when the monster, as a metaphor or myth, is conflated with the reality of a modern world in which humankind is increasingly self-conscious and alienated from its predetermined social structures.[8]

Certainly, Hitchcock was not the first to suggest monstrosity and society are sides of the same coin nor did he invent the idea of situating these themes cinematically within the domestic coordinates of rural and suburban America. In the 1950s, films like *The Night of the Hunter* (1955) and *Invasion of the Body Snatchers* (1956) had decisively located monstrosity in everyday American society, but *Psycho* did lend the motif of monstrosity within the family home an unprecedented status. While the film marks a significant turning point in the development of the horror genre, Jancovich insists that its release cannot fully account for the structural and thematic changes that occur in the decades that follow: "this concern with the family and with the instability of identity ... was to become one of the central problems within contemporary horror. It cannot simply be explained as the innovation of *Psycho*, or its director Alfred Hitchcock. It was part of a more general cultural process."[9]

If, indeed, the link between American society and the monstrous has long been the cornerstone of serious discussions of the modern horror film, then the category of the "social thriller" is a tautology, but no less a curious one. The difficulty Peele expresses in trying to place his film within the coordinates of the horror genre stems not from a lack of familiarity with its patterns for organizing narrative conflicts or its dominant themes and character types, but rather, I would submit, results from his knowing them too well. In other words, Peele's knowledge of the genre produces the very epistemological rupture he satirizes ("it's a documentary") then later seeks to reconcile through the invention of a new generic category ("it's a social thriller").

This brings us back to the signifying power of Blackness. When Peele describes his trouble categorizing *Get Out*, what he is really saying is he is trying to come to terms with how to integrate Black protagonism into a genre that has historically excluded Black narrative agency except in the outlier cases of Romero's *Night of the Living Dead*, 1970s Blaxploitation horror films like *Blacula* (1972) and *Blackenstein* (1973), or art-house anomalies like Bill Gunn's *Ganja and Hess* (1973) and what seems to me its remake, Claire Denis's *Trouble Every Day* (2001). Far from being merely a derivative turn or a satirical portrayal of Blackness, what horror films from Blaxploitation cinema to the horror parodies of the late 1990s/early 2000s register is how Blackness in the cultural imaginary is generically comprehensible only within inflexible and highly restricted narrative positions. This much discussed and generalized confusion over how to categorize *Get Out* is unmistakably fused to the Blackness of the film's protagonist. It is so unusual and unexpected to see a Black man as a lead character in a horror film—that is not explicitly a satire or comedy—that when the trailer for the film was first released, the bizarre narrative proposition it offered caused many (myself included) to immediately take notice.

The theatrical trailer for *Get Out* was released on October 4, 2016. It begins with a young Black man opening the door to his apartment and kissing his white girlfriend who has come to pick him up for a weekend visit to her parent's home in the suburbs. The image of a young, interracial couple in a Hollywood film would be cause enough for arrest as it comes freighted with a deep history of racist representations dating back to the emergence of Hollywood narrative cinema itself, but that the trailer appeared to be advertising a horror film with a Black lead was equally, if not more stunning. Describing her own astonishment at seeing the film's trailer, film historian Tananarive Due writes,

> … in the fall of 2016, I sat, mouth agape, watching the trailer for an upcoming horror film called *Get Out*. It had a black protagonist, was addressing race in ways both obvious and subtle, and it showed a black child sinking through his bed and into the floor into what I would later learn was a quietly revolutionary concept called the sunken place.[10]

In reactions on social media forums one could gauge a common feeling that the trailer was promoting something out of the ordinary. On the Black popular culture video site Worldstarhiphop.com, responding to the trailer, one commenter declares, "FINALLY! A horror movie with an

African American lead." Another quips, "What if the black man doesn't even survive this one though?" Several comments also underscore the problem of genre: "Watch the trailer the first time, it looks like a horror movie, watch again and it's a comedy." Similarly, one commenter asks, "So is this a black comedy or what?" To which another commenter replies, "Black Horror." Finally, another comment reads, "Well, well, well … if this Brother ain't smart enough to see the signs and listen to his partners, then he deserves what he gets. Plus, you already know he ain't gonna make it outta that compound. Dead man walking … ." Most of the comments (2536 at time of writing) responding to the film's trailer all share this tone of surprise, confusion, and certainty in how the film will inevitably end for its Black lead.[11]

In short, Blackness elevated to the role of lead protagonist (even in the fragment of a movie trailer) in a horror film does not simply subvert audience expectations or disrupt the rituals of viewership and participation the genre mandates, it short-circuits the paradigm altogether. Black horror parodies notwithstanding, when a Black protagonist is dying, dies, or is undead, Black agency can logically be assimilated into the generic economy of the American horror film. Alternatively, a Black protagonist surviving the monster's onslaught and living until the final image fades and the credits role is so unprecedented even Peele himself cannot come to terms with the narrative proposition his own film affords. Little wonder then why a horror film with a Black protagonist, Black characters, and a few fleeting moments of humor would reflexively be deemed a comedy, even from its prospective audience after seeing only a promotional trailer. From the *Scary Movie* cycle and its lesser Wayans Brothers helmed spin-off *A Haunted House* (2013) and *A Haunted House 2* (2014); from *Leprechaun in the Hood* (2000) and *Leprechaun: Back to Tha Hood* (2003) to Tyler Perry's *Boo! A Medea Halloween* (2016) and Boo 2! (2017), the tone of Black contributions to the genre has historically not been one of seriousness or legitimacy, but rather parody and self-deprecation. Subverting parodic expectations of Blackness in Hollywood horror films is *Get Out*'s first masterstroke and the categorical confusion around the film attests to how deeply representations of Blackness in the genre remain bonded to narrative protocols of folly and buffoonery.

It will come as little surprise that the generic illegibility of Black protagonism in horror is deeply entangled with histories of anti-Black racism in Hollywood. The various confusions *Get Out* inspires around race and categorical placement throws light on the structural exclusion of Blacks from playing certain character types in genres that have traditionally been reserved for white actors portraying white characters. Admittedly, the subject of systemic racism in Hollywood and tracking its obdurate arc goes well beyond what can be adequately addressed here, but it is important to note that *Get Out*'s release coincides with the social justice siren calls of #TimesUp and #OscarsSoWhite, both respectively advocating for gender and racial parity in the film industry. Recounting the impact of #OscarsSoWhite, a *New York Times* article titled "The Hashtag That Changed the Oscars: An Oral History" maps out how the hashtag began trending on the morning of January 15, 2015, after all twenty Oscar nominations in acting categories went to white performers for the second consecutive year. Through snippets of oral testimony from industry insiders like Spike Lee, Ava DuVernay, Cheryl Boone Isaacs, and others, pop-culture reporter Reggie Udwu describes how it appeared the film industry was taking seriously calls for racial equity after Steve McQueen's *12 Years a Slave* (2013) was awarded the Best Picture Oscar in 2014. But the ensuing years saw a retrenchment of the small gains made toward expanding Black productions, spotlighting diverse talent, and bolstering racial inclusion in Hollywood.

On the following morning of January 16, 2015, the front page of the *Los Angeles Times* read, "Where's the Diversity?" alongside the faces of each of the white nominees for acting awards. The growing backlash against the Academy's nominations triggered an emergency meeting of its board of governors who "approved ambitious targets for a membership initiative known as A2020, aiming to double the number of women and ethnically underrepresented members in four years."[12] This accelerated effort to diversify all areas of the Hollywood film industry serves as the backdrop to Jordan Peele's feature directorial debut with a film about a Black man who endures every imaginable form of liberal racism en route to indefinite physical and psychic bondage. Curiously, though, over the course of these wide-ranging debates on genre and classification what has passed largely without comment—even from its writer/director—is the film's close affiliation in tone and structure to one subgenre in particular: *torture porn*.

Torture Porn

In a 2006 article for *New York* magazine, David Edelstein coins the term "torture porn" to describe an emergent trend in American horror films characterized by acute brutality and a fascination with the grisly minutiae of torture and mutilation. Pointing to the release of horror films like *Saw* (2004), *The Devil's Rejects* (2005), *Hostel* (2005), and *Wolf Creek* (2005), Edelstein muses openly on what might be the attraction for American audiences to see the explicit visualization of violence on screen protracted to unwatchable limits. "Some of these movies are so viciously nihilistic that the only point seems to be to force you to suspend moral judgments," writes Edelstein who sees in horror films after 9/11 the collapse of a moral binary at the level of identification where aligning one's sympathies with victims or violators becomes increasingly unclear.[13] While the article is right to point out that representations of violence in American cinema—and in mainstream media more generally— have long been trending in the direction of explicitness, it misses some nuance on what makes torture porn distinctive from other exceedingly violent horror films like the B-movie Exploitation horror films of the 1970s and Indie slasher films of the 1980s.

In *Torture Porn in the Wake of 9/11: Horror, Exploitation, and the Cinema of Sensation* film scholar Aaron Michael Kerner helps clarify this area of inquiry by identifying the key tropes that have come to define torture porn. Kerner finds that:

1 Torture porn films are always based in reality. Horror is not an external phenomenon, it is more intimately a part of us and caused by us: "Torture porn, perhaps more so than any incarnation of the horror genre before it, starkly vivifies this idea."[14]

2 Victims are abducted before they are tortured or killed.

3 Domestic homes double as torture facilities.

4 Victims struck by the randomness and inexplicability of their abduction and the violence they are subjected to ask questions like "Why are you doing this?" or "What did I ever do to you?"

5 Victims are rebirthed from the womb of the torture chamber after they escape.

6 Torture porn narratives are structured around gaming motifs and Big Game hunting.

7 Abductors use video to moralize their violence. Flashbacks offering background information on abductors and/or victims tend also to be mediated through video. Torture porn films allow spectators to feel the weight of history.

8 Camera flashes are a common trope in torture porn films, typically serving as an editing device.

9 The intentions of violators are never purely "evil" in the religious sense of the word. They can always be explained through their moral imperatives or capitalist pursuits.

I raise the conventions of torture porn in relation to *Get Out* not to try to resolve the tension around its generic categorization (I do not believe this is a tension easily resolved) by decidedly declaring it as such; however, in the close critical race reading that follows, even in the absence of graphic scenes of bodily undoing common in torture porn films, it will become clear that its core themes and plot devices show it to be patently one of them. The point I wish to emphasize is that Black protagonism in the horror film appears to shift otherwise recognizable conventions into a critical blind spot. From horror to comedy, from social thriller to torture porn, the generic elasticity of *Get Out* proves amenable to a wide swath of Hollywood genres and this phenomenon, I maintain, is directly attributable to the destabilizing effect of the *final brother*.

It seems to me not coincidental that the blueprint for the torture porn film mapped out through the tropes Kerner identifies lends itself readily to a film about neo-slavery and social death in which Black bodies are stolen, sold, and stripped of their subjectivity. At its core, torture porn shows how human beings are rendered superfluous in a machinery of unchecked bourgeois curiosity with its inexhaustible fixation on mastering the intractability of life and death. It makes clear how the destruction of human uniqueness—an event that torture in all permutations does not bring about contingently, but one it resolutely pursues—in torture porn turns bodies into commodities that are expendable not only physically, but ontologically as well.

The commodification of bodies is, in fact, so essential to torture porn narratives it constitutes its guiding imperative. In the *Hostel* series (2005–11), young tourists in European cities are abducted and auctioned off to bidders vying for the opportunity to maim, mutilate, and murder their winnings. Similarly, *Turistas* (2006) tells the story of backpackers vacationing in a rural region of Brazil before they are abducted by criminals who harvest their organs and sell them on the black market. In Pascal Laugier's underappreciated 2008 film *Martyrs*, women are captured, tortured, and pushed to the brink of death with the hope they will enter the liminal space between living and dying and share their transcendental findings with the wealthy patrons funding this macabre undertaking. As recently as the summer of 2021 in *Don't Breathe 2*, drug dealers conspire to kidnap a teenage girl and surgically remove her heart so that it can be transplanted into her estranged, dying mother whose skill as a narcotic "cook" is crucial to the success of their illicit business. In these films and many more like them, the abduction of bodies to be shredded, garroted, dismembered, or flayed for purposes of pleasure or profit is frequently linked to a shadow economy where crime and privilege are indistinguishable along the path of life, liberty, and the pursuit of happiness.

In torture porn films an individual or organization always profits (or attempts to profit), in some way, from the corporeal disintegration of others. Put plainly, the conventional torture porn narrative would not make sense, nor would its conflicts or the means and ends of its violence be tenable, outside the context of neoliberal capitalism and consumerist excess. We see this in the ways these films foreground the desires that fuel capitalist consumption (albeit in the extreme) and how they invariably lead to feelings of dissatisfaction that paradoxically appear resolvable only through further accumulation and consumption at the expense of others and, even more radically, oneself. Naturally, *Get Out* extends this capitalist logic in the allusions it makes to the transatlantic slave trade and how it portrays Black bodies as fungible commodities. Thus, on the question of genre, the torture porn film would appear to be tailor-made for a story about the perpetuation of Black indentured servitude through the capture, sale, and surgical manipulation of Black bodies made into psychic vessels for wealthy white people. By adding Blackness and subtracting torture, and utilizing not some, but all its tropes, *Get Out* proves to be both a watershed example of Black horror and a unique variation on the torture porn film that significantly modifies the paradigm.

"Creepy, Confusing-ass Subuuurb"

In the opening scene of *Get Out*, a Black man is walking alone in an upper-middle class suburban neighborhood at night. Trees and post lamps line the moonlit street. The grass is manicured and the hedges are meticulously trimmed. The camera gradually dollies back as Andre (Lakeith Stanfield) steps into the frame. Almost immediately we hear a dog bark at him off-screen as if to signal not only is he unwelcome in the neighborhood, but he is intruding on the composition of the frame itself. He casts nervous glances left and right. He is lost and tells his cellphone companion, "I feel like a sore thumb out here." The person he is speaking to on the phone shares directions, then Andre ends the call. He nervously talks to himself as he tries to find his bearings. Soon a vintage white Porsche drives past and U-turns to pull up alongside of him. Andre recites a familiar mantra in everyday Black life when faced with being Black in the wrong place at the wrong time: "Ok. I just keep on walking. Don't do nuthin' stupid, just keep walking." As the car continues creeping behind him, he decides, "Fuck this, imma fuckin' go the other way I came. Not today. Not me. You know how they do muthafuckas out here, man, I'm gone." Andre turns and walks in the other direction and as he moves to cross the street, he notices that the driver side door of the white Porsche is now open. Not a moment later, a person in black clothing and a black helmet steps out of the dark and chokes Andre unconscious before stuffing his limp body in the trunk of the car.

In this scene the camera does not come to meet Andre as he steps on to the sidewalk to move astride trimmed hedges, white picket fences and detached family homes. Instead, the camera dollies back, away from Andre as he enters the frame seemingly uninvited. The sense of intrusion into this suburban neighborhood is thus doubled at the level of film form. Of course, there is nothing about Andre's comportment or any action of his in particular that marks his presence as intrusive; it is simply that Andre is a Black man in a neighborhood that is coded white. We never see any of the residents of this street but we know who lives in these houses, and we know exactly why Andre is "creeped" out by being there, and, moreover, why he does not seem able to navigate its "confusing-ass" terrain. As the media critic Ryan Poll points out, "This opening shot reverses the racist logic that if you see a Black man walking at night, the correct affect is 'fear' and the correct instinct is 'flight.' Instead, and more truthfully, it is Black men who should be afraid while walking alone in a White zone."[15] This fear of coded white spaces is common among Black characters in the horror genre. The documentary *Horror Noire* (2019), which admirably tracks the history of Blacks in horror films, begins with film directors Rusty Cundieff (*Tales from the Hood*) and Ernest Dickerson (*Juice*) sitting in a movie theater watching this opening scene from *Get Out*. Dickerson says to Cundieff, "Walking down the sidewalk in a suburban neighborhood … by himself. Shit, I been there." Dickerson concludes, "It was the perfect Black horror story."

The scene of a potential victim walking through an unfamiliar neighborhood at night and feeling tense or anxious about being out of place is not uncommon in the American horror film, but in *Get Out* this comes with an added racial supplement. For the Black person walking through an upper-middle class neighborhood the fear is that their Blackness will mark them not only as out of place, but as a potential threat; that Blackness itself is the mark of something irreducibly threatening and monstrous. The camera dollying back along the sidewalk recalls similar eerie and unsettling shots from films like John Carpenter's *Halloween* (1978) and David Lynch's *Blue Velvet* (1986). The difference is one of belonging. In these films there is never a question if the protagonists *belong* in the suburban spaces in which we find them. When Sandy Williams and Jeffrey Beaumont walk through a dark, suburban neighborhood at night, never is there a feeling that they are out of place. Even as they pass a white man wearing sunglasses in the dead of night while walking his dog, nothing seems too far out of the ordinary. When Laurie and friends are roaming the streets of Haddonfield, never is there a sense that they do not belong where we find them. The immediate tension that *Get Out* sets up develops precisely out of questions of race and spatial belonging.

As a point of contrast, take an early scene from *Ganja and Hess*. The film's protagonist, Dr. Hess Green, is entertaining a dinner guest—George Meda—who, after becoming inebriated, wanders out into the night. Hess finds his guest sitting on a tree branch and next to him hanging from an adjacent branch is a noose. The companion tells Green that he should not take his attempt to commit suicide by hanging personally as it has nothing to do with him. Hess replies: "It has nothing to do with me? But you see, it is my tree and my rope. And that would give the authorities the right to invade my privacy with all sorts of embarrassing questions." "I tried not to involve you," Mr. Meda insists, to which Hess replies, "Mr. Meda, there's no possible way for you to know this, but I am the only colored on the block, you see. And if another Black man washes ashore around here you can believe the authorities will drag me out for questioning." More than four decades later, *Get Out* begins by emphasizing the fact that in American horror films, issues of race and space remain inseparable.

Staying Woke and the White Gaze

The film's opening credits sequence introduces Chris Washington and Rose Armitage (Allison Williams)—the film's interracial couple—while hinting at several key themes that will echo across the film's narrative arc. Subtly woven into these establishing shots are the dramas of Black predation and racial code switching, the power of the white gaze, and the objectification and commodification of Blackness that lends the film its dramatic thrust. This sequence—what I call the "Stay Woke" sequence after the repeated refrain in the Childish Gambino song "Redbone" heard on the soundtrack, and for the premonitory allusions it makes—is comprised of twenty shots beginning with a short montage and a pair of tracking shots that reveal large monochrome photographs on the walls of Chris' apartment (a pregnant mother in front of a housing project, a bird in flight, a child holding a mask up to his/her face). As the camera creeps toward the bathroom the image of the child with the mask gives way to the image of Chris' reflection in the bathroom mirror. Fresh out of the shower, Chris wipes moisture from the mirror and applies white shaving cream across his cheeks and mouth (what amounts to wearing a mask of a different kind) before we cut to Rose in a bakery buying pastries. We see Rose's face from inside the glass display case as she peruses her options. Framed in medium-close-up she surveys the pastries with a wry smile. Through subtle allusion we are introduced here for the first time to the power of the *white gaze* as her eyes move from one option to the next. We cut back to Chris whose face is fully lathered as he begins to shave. With each stroke of the razor the black skin hidden beneath the white "mask" reappears until he accidentally cuts himself. Stung by the pain, Chris pauses momentarily to locate the cut and stop the bleeding by applying pressure to it with his finger. In the shots that follow, Chris, now fully dressed, is cycling through photographs on his camera; Rose, holding bags of pastries and coffee, arrives at Chris' front door; they kiss before she enters his apartment, then he closes the door.

This sequence metaphorizes a moment of Black self-recognition in a white world and the calculated racial switching that is often necessary if white worlds are to be navigated safely and successfully. It is also, thematically, the axis on which the entire story spins. First, through parallel editing, Peele binds Chris and Chris' double in the mirror to Rose's white gaze. In the previous chapter, I explained how the white gaze is a visual field of power that presumes everything that appears before it can be owned, possessed, and eventually consumed. Peele suggests in his arrangement of shots that among the objects held by Rose's white gaze scanning the glass display case is also Chris' body and his identity (doubled in the mirror). It should not go ignored that the camera is itself an instrument for inscribing the power of the white gaze and so it is all the more ironic that the first time we see Chris outside of the bathroom and dressed he is holding a camera and looking through images he has taken. While he may possess the camera he is holding he does not wield its inscriptive power. After all, he is, as we will come to learn, a photographer whose images circulate for purchase on the art market.

There is a generative connection to be made between Chris applying the white mask of shaving cream to his face and the trans/plantationary logic that underwrites Blackface minstrelsy. In Blackface performance the minstrel mask served as a screen behind which whites could assume the identity of Blacks and "affectionately" mimic Blackness in exaggerated song and dance. The Blackface mask functioned for whites as a conduit affording another degree of mastery over both the Black body and the involuntary feelings it inspires including fear, fascination, repulsion, love, and desire.[16] It also served a competing purpose by permitting an imaginary form of racial mixing whereby whites, in the masquerade of Blackness, could "embody" and thus contain the libidinal excess of the Black body. As Raengo points out, "Leveraging the expected mimetic relation between skin color and racial identity, blackface minstrelsy turns the epidermal signifier into a man-made mask. The mask in turn authorizes a performance of Blackness. The possibility of doing Blackness highlights the idea of appropriation, which is only available if Blackness is at least somewhat performative already."[17] I want to suggest that a similar, though inverted, performance—or at least an attempt at performance—is at play in the Stay Woke sequence when Chris applies the white shaving cream to his face. Chris' "whiting up" hints at the racial code switching he will need to perform (indeed, that he is *preparing* to perform) over the weekend to come. In contrast to the affordances of buffoonery and merriment in Blackface minstrelsy and the impunity white people have historically had to toggle freely between epidermal signifiers, whiteness is not performative in the way Blackness is.

It is worth recalling here what Saidiya Hartman tells us about the abstractness, immateriality and fungibility of the commodity, and how Blackness in an economy of pleasure "enabled the Black body or blackface mask to serve as the vehicle of white self-exploration, renunciation, and enjoyment."[18] Chris cutting his face while removing the white mask is a subtle but potent metaphor that suggests cultural appropriations fail when reversed. White to Black inhabitations have and remain open modes of exploration and possibility for whites, but Black to white inhabitations, as *Get Out* shows us, end frequently in failure, embarrassment, exposure, or more immediately, pain.

Peele's decision to use Gambino's "Redbone" in the introduction to the film's interracial couple cleverly underscores the deep-seated cultural anxieties attached to interracial relationships between Black men and white women. Again, in the refrain of the song we hear:

> But stay woke
> Niggas creepin'
> They gon' find you
> Gon' catch you sleepin' (oh)
> Now stay woke
> Niggas creepin'
> Now don't you close your eyes

Here woke conjugates both a present and future tense. The lyrics of the refrain serve as a stern warning that there are people scheming in secret. The line, "Gon' catch you sleepin'" also foreshadows the hypnotic state Chris will be plunged into in Missy Armitage's office. In Black vernacular, "Gon' catch you sleepin'" means that if you relax vigilance or do not remain conscious of your surroundings or the circumstances you are in, people will take advantage of you. The declarative "stay woke" presumes one is already in a state of being woke and attention should be paid to the people, places and things that might unseat you from your wokeness. This may seem overly rhetorical, but it can be gainfully observed from the vantage point of the film's third act to be a stern, extra-diegetic warning to Chris.[19] It also doubles as a warning (or better yet, a knowing elbow-nudge) to the film's Black audience about the dangers involved when entering interracial relationships—a point Chris' best friend Rod will repeatedly reinforce throughout the film.

"Do they know I'm Black?"

As Chris packs his weekend bag, Rose senses he is troubled by something that he is not expressing. When she presses Chris to share, he replies: "Do they know I'm Black?" This question and Chris feeling the need to pose the question to Rose reveals an important dimension of racialized self-perception. In advance of Rose's response to the question "Do they know I'm Black?" we know with certainty that even if it is the case that his liberal, white girlfriend has parents who share in her seemingly progressive worldview, Chris is not colorblind to his Blackness and cannot extricate himself from his own awareness of his status as a racialized subject. Evoking again the metaphor from the previous sequence, the man in the mirror, as it were, is irreducibly Black and racial code switching from Black to white and back again can be painful. As a Black man who is all-too conscious of his Blackness and what it signifies, Chris' concerns confirm the deception underlying claims for post-racial subjectivity.

The question "Do they know I'm Black?" also taps into the long history of miscegenation in America. When Chris tells Rose "You said I'm the first Black guy you ever dated. I just don't want to be chased off the lawn with a shotgun," he is referring to well-documented episodes of racial terror and intimidation on the ledger of American history. From Emmett Till, who was lynched and brutally murdered for speaking to a white woman, to O.J. Simpson's so-called "Trial of the Century" for the alleged murder of his white wife (Nicole Brown Simpson) and its deep re-inscription of the color line across all areas of American society in the early 1990s, the dramas of miscegenation have served as anchor points for one of Hollywood cinema's perennial depictions of Black sociality.

Little more need be added to the voluminous accounts of race mixing on record, or how representations of miscegenation in Hollywood cinema are often the projections of a white imaginary both terrified and fascinated by the mythic sexual potency of the Black body, or that the scenes of miscegenation that have organized the presence of Black life on screen are narratives that have been perpetuated by a commercial industry that has historically registered Blackness in three distinct ways: as servile and subservient, as comedic or musical merriment, or as threatening. In this context we can designate *Get Out* as another waypoint in the long, obdurate arc of screen representations of miscegenation in Hollywood cinema from *Birth of a Nation* (1915) to *Jungle Fever* (1991), and beyond.

Rose placates Chris' fears by assuring him that her father "would have voted for Obama for a third time if he could have." This is really just another version of the all-too familiar colorblind claim, "I have Black friends, so how can I be racist?" As we come to discover that the family not only shares in generational legacies of racism but is also perpetuating forms of racial terror and bodily seizure that underwrites the whole history of American life, the bundle of assurances Rose offers Chris are worth unpacking. Embedded in the claim that her parents are not racist and that they would have voted for Obama a third time if the rules of multi-term presidential elections were possible is the suggestion that racism is something easily recognizable (recalling Justice Potter Stewart's well-known remarks on pornography: "I know it when I see it").

The idea that racism is always identifiable is the rebar of both neoliberal and neoconservative fantasies around racial discrimination. The idea is that if I am not using racial epithets or openly discriminating others because of skin color, vocal accents, or other markers of difference to the hegemonic norms of white America, then I am not a racist. Of course, the term *microaggressions* was invented expressly for the purpose of naming and elucidating how racism, particularly "soft" racism (in many ways, more insidious than explicit "hard" racism) is only nameable from the subject position of the addressed, not the addressee. It also comes as little surprise that Rose should elect to invoke the figure of Barack Obama as the sedative to soothe Chris' anxieties. The very idea of Obama is so heavily freighted with egalitarian notions of post-racial fraternity that the mere mention of his name means to express in shorthand whole-scale erasures of epidermal difference. "Do they know I'm Black?" is in a sense then the obverse formulation of the question posed in the title of the classic Sidney Portier film *Guess Who's Coming to Dinner?* (1967). The answer, of course, is the same answer Rose rhetorically offers Chris in jest: "Mom and Dad, my Black boyfriend will be coming up this weekend and I just don't want you to be shocked that he's … a Black man."

The remainder of the film's first act is composed in four segments designed by Peele to openly pressure test Chris' capacity for enduring racial stereotyping and microaggressions. In these narrative segments, Chris has an exchange with a police officer, he meets the Armitage family, has dinner with the Armitages and meets Rose's brother Jeremy, then finally ends the day in bed with Rose. While we see Chris deftly navigating the racial minefield of traveling into the "subuuurbs" (as Andre put it) and spending time with his white girlfriend's family at their home, a web of deception, one in which he is already caught, is slowly being spun.

"Can I see your ID?"

In the first segment we are introduced to Rod, Chris' best friend. Chris and Rose begin their drive to her parent's home in the suburbs when Chris calls Rod—a TSA agent—to go over his housesitting duties for the weekend. Rod speaks briefly to Rose and they share a joking flirtation: "You know you picked the wrong guy, right?" It is a moment that seems innocuous in its levity, but will serve as a critical narrative device later in the film after Rod loses touch with Chris and suspects that Rose and her family may have done something to him. Before they end the conversation, Rod reminds Chris of a basic "rule" for interracial relationships: "Don't go to a white girl's parent's house," a warning that will prove prescient before the film reaches its climax. Chris ignores Rod, and ends the call.

Peele, who is one half of *Key and Peele* (2012–15), the successful comedy sketch-show created with friend and writing partner Keegan-Michael Key, has been a comedy writer for television going back to his first credit on the comedy series *MADtv* in 2003. For his first feature length script, Peele co-wrote the comedy *Keanu* (2016), the story of a slacker who has his kitten kidnapped and is forced to enter into the world of urban gangsterism to get it back. It is not at all surprising that Peele's comedic sensibilities would inform the tone of his first horror film or that a character like Rod would play a prominent role in the story's development. Black characters in horror films often function at the narrative level as comedic relief from the rising tension between the monster and the horror film's real protagonists, its white characters—white women in particular. Rod fulfills this role by adding mirth to the gravity of Chris' predicament while doubling as Chris' anchor to the outside world.

In Chapter 1, I described how the Black body, police brutality, the perpetuation of racial logics rooted in the obliterative universe of chattel slavery, and the myriad ways the American police state operates as an extension of (not so) veiled white supremacist ideology, are key issues in contemporary critical race theory. These tensions first emerge in an encounter Rose and Chris have with a police officer after accidentally striking a doe crossing the road with their car. The officer on the scene is speaking to Rose and taking down her account of the accident before calling to Chris to produce his driver's license. Chris, lost in thought (thoughts we will later learn are no doubt connected to his mother who was killed in a hit and run accident when he was a child), motions to comply before Rose reminds the officer that Chris was not driving the car. Rose resists the officer's request while Chris pliantly removes his "state ID" from his wallet to present to the officer. As Rose continues her protest police dispatch contacts the officer over CB radio and asks if everything is alright. This is a pivotal moment at the level of both narrative and visual representation. If the officer responds to dispatch by requesting back up, the situation, despite its routineness, could potentially escalate into a life and death matter for Chris (who, as we soon come to learn, is already locked in a matter of life and death, or more precisely, being and non-being). As we have seen time and time again in amateur video recordings of police arrests of Black people the risk of being shot or otherwise killed remains open whether one complies by reaching into a pocket to retrieve the very documents being requested, or whether one is merely lying motionless face down and obeying the commands being issued (or even if you are Black and having a picnic in a public park or out for a jog). When the officer pauses briefly, then responds begrudgingly to the radio inquiry with "No, everything is fine," we know with some certainty that a potentially lethal situation for Chris, lethal for no other reason than his Blackness, has been averted (and yet, ironically, permitting the real lethality of his predicament to continue). It is a brief moment of loaded tension in the film predicated entirely upon the audience's familiarity with encounters between Black men and law enforcement officers and how they tend too often to result in the death of a Black man being shot or strangled.

In the opening scene from *The Hate U Give (THUG)* (2018), Maverick, a Black man, is seated at a small dining table with his wife and three children (Starr, Seven, and Sekani) and he is giving them "the talk." "The talk" lays out a set of protocols Black people must abide by when they encounter police during a traffic stop. He explains that their hands should always be in plain sight on the dashboard, and that they should not argue and cooperate by remaining calm and motionless because it could get "dangerous," but not offer more information than what is asked of them. Starr's internal narration interrupts "the talk" to note that she is age nine, and her brothers ten and one. Maverick ends "the talk" by insisting that they not allow law enforcement's treatment of Black life to lessen their sense of self-worth.

To watch a Black father have to explain to his children that being Black in America requires that they recognize their Blackness marks them as potential targets of state sanctioned violence, and to then rehearse with them the theatrics of survival is an absolutely devastating scene. The film, as expected, pivots on a moment when Starr, years later, is in the passenger seat of a car with a friend (a young Black man) who is pulled over by police and is eventually shot and killed when the police mistake the hairbrush in his hand for a gun.

When Chris acquiesces to the police officer's request to see his identification, he is executing (at least, in principle) the protocols of "the talk." As he makes his way toward the officer to surrender his identification for inspection, Rose says, "No, fuck that, you don't have to give him your ID because you didn't do anything wrong." Chris calmly repeats that he is fine with showing his identification, but Rose is adamant in standing her ground, as it were, and declining the officer's command. The officer notes that standard operating procedure requires that he examine identification from all parties present at the scene of an accident, but Rose bluntly replies: "Bullshit." Rose, an attractive, young white woman, and the white officer share a loaded look and finally the officer returns her driver's license and tells her to "Fix that headlight, and that mirror," before walking back to his patrol car. Rose concludes the encounter with a mildly sarcastic "Thank you, officer."

Needless to say, the affordances available to Rose in this situation are utterly foreclosed to Chris as almost every move she makes flagrantly defies the protocols of "the talk" Black parents must relay to their children if they hope to survive run-ins with the police. The divide here between white and Black life in the context of law enforcement is stark. It is an absurd bit of fantasia to imagine Chris reciting Rose's lines to the officer and expecting the same result. Chris' response is not a spontaneous reaction to a situation, but a set of trained responses necessary for Black people to navigate potentially lethal encounters with agents of "law enforcement."

In the following scene, Chris compliments Rose on her audaciousness, to which she replies, "I'm not going to let anyone fuck with my man." But it is worth noting another incentive behind Rose insisting that Chris not turn over his identification. She is acutely aware that there will likely be a report filed for a missing person after Chris is auctioned and the Coagula process is completed. By preventing the officer from seeing Chris' state ID, Rose averts the possibility of the officer placing Chris' name into an accident report and establishing a paper trail back to her and the Armitage family after Chris is, in no uncertain terms, abducted and enslaved.

Worlds of White Privilege

The traffic stop and the tension with law enforcement make clear that the moment Chris leaves his home, he is left with no alternative but to recognize himself as a racialized subject. There is more than a little irony in the fact that before Chris has even arrived at the Armitage home where he will be hypnotized, auctioned off, and rendered a passenger in his own body, he is already made into a spectator to stand by and watch Rose and the police officer decide if he will or will not turnover his identification for inspection. This is the first moment in the film where we see white privilege in action. White privilege is always first and foremost freedom: the freedom to go where one wishes, say what one feels to whomever one wishes to speak, to take possession of what one wants, and to refuse legal injunctions put forth by law enforcement officers with near impunity and without fear of reprisal.

As Rose and Chris drive up to the front door of the Armitage home they pass by the Black groundskeeper raking leaves alongside the driveway. After parking the car they are greeted at the door by Rose's parents, Dean Armitage (Bradley Whitford) and Missy Armitage (Catherine Keener). Dean excitedly tells Chris, "Call me Dean, my man, and give me a hug." The phrase "my man" is the same phrase used in the car by Rose just before they arrive at the house. Using "borrowed language" Dean attempts to convey fraternity while tapping into Black "coolness," something Dean will again be guilty of when moments later he asks Rose and Chris, "So how long has it been going on ... this *thang*?"

When Dean takes Chris on a tour of the estate he shows Chris various objects and possessions that decorate the Armitage family home. This tour suggests that white privilege is rooted in colonialist logic. The objects are all emblems of access and unimpeded movement into other cultural and geographic spaces. If the colonialist project has at its core the occupation of alien territories and staking claim to things (objects, land, persons, culture itself) to which it has no rightful claim, the Armitage home is colonialist fantasy through and through. Various objects and ephemera acquired abroad line the hallways and adorn the walls. Dean quips, "It's such a privilege to experience another person's culture." This privilege Dean speaks of often frames its seizing of things or leveraging its advantages as achievements or accomplishments. In even more grotesque forms, white privilege frames its dominion over things and others in magnanimous terms (civilizing the savage, indoctrinating the "ignorant," cultural preservation, etc.).

Here the Armitage home and Chris' apartment are set in stark contrast. Where on Chris' walls there are only scenes of urban life captured from behind the barrier of a camera's lens—images distanced and impersonal—on the walls of the Armitage home are photos of generational kinship and family unity. Like puzzle pieces being moved into place to construct a larger portrait of the privilege of which Dean speaks, he points to a photograph of his son Jeremy who is in medical school to "be just like his old man." Jeremy, like Rose, has been sucked into the jetstream of generational wealth where family money and the power it confers will allow him to seamlessly carry forward the family's patriarchal legacy. Dean then shows Chris a photograph of his father in a sprinter's pose and explains that he was beaten by Jesse Owens in the qualifying round of the Berlin Olympics in 1936. Owens (a Black athlete) went on to win the gold medal in the 100M Sprint in front of Adolf Hitler who had hoped to use the Games as a transfer point to advance his theory of eugenics from philosophy to reality. "Tough break for your Dad," Chris says to Dean, to which he ruminatively replies, "Yeah. He almost got over it."

As it turns out, this experience for Grandpa Armitage is the anchoring point of the entire Coagula operation. For the elder Armitage the loss to Owens was perceived as an insurmountable biological obstacle. His response to the problem of beating Owens is colonialist logic *par excellence*: if I cannot manifest what I want with what I have, I will alter the structure of the "field of play" and take what I wish from the other by force. The German media covering the Berlin Olympics referred to Black athletes as "black auxiliaries." An auxiliary is a supplement or a form of additional support, typically of foreign origin, to an established order or dominant system. It is no coincidence that Grandpa Armitage should have devised a medical procedure that literally transforms Black bodies into auxiliaries for white consciousness. Worlds of white privilege bend everything in its ambit to meet its desires. Again, it is life, liberty and the pursuit of happiness, but always at the other's expense.

When Chris is later asked by Missy Armitage where his parents are, Chris lays out an all-too familiar paradigm of young Black life being raised in a fatherless home with a single mother. For privilege to pass easily into innocuousness it must appear to be simply the way things are. The very act of being able to frame photographs and adorn walls with these minor icons to blood bonds and family ties is itself a privileged act. These forms of domestic adornment are alien to those raised in conditions where kinship structures are never visibly whole, unified, or traceable. While this is not necessarily a gesture that plays out unilaterally along color lines, in the context of the visual logic of the film it brings into focus why the photos we see on the walls of Chris' apartment are images of his own making and not family photos. It also helps to establish what makes Chris a suitable candidate for abduction. The idea here, to borrow a phrase from Winston Wolf, the problem solver in Quentin Tarantino's *Pulp Fiction* (1994) called upon to dispose of a dead Black body, is that "No one will be missed."

Chris, his father absent and his mother deceased, appears in the film to have no one in his life but Rod, his best friend, and Rose, his girlfriend whom he believes loves and cares for him. This is where the film's true emotional demolition lies. It offers a portrait of a Black life that has endured and survived trauma, and knows intimately the rootlessness and abyssal depths of a life without the love of a father and the lost love of a mother. I want to stress this latter point for it is one many young Black people must endure and it is an experience so shattering that it requires a lifetime of erecting emotional barriers, strategies of affective displacement, and cautious, guarded relations to others indefinitely for fear of further abandonment. As Chris will learn, Rose will not only cast him back into abandonment, she has already gauged the depth of this traumatic reservoir in order to assess his suitability for the Coagula procedure and, in turn, underwrite his candidacy for capture.

This might explain why Rose and the Armitage family employ the methods they use to select and seize their victims. It is a process that ultimately aims, over time, to psychologically breakdown their captives and to render them vulnerable and less willing or able to fight back. To the question "How long has it been going on, this *thang*?" Rose replies, "five months." This extended period of acquaintance seems necessary for the process to take hold. Over this time, victims form an intimate attachment to Rose who no doubt learns as much as she can about their traumatic experiences and relays this information back to her parents who then prepare to identify the psychological fissures that might break open their psyche and render them vulnerable to hypnotic suggestion.

The Field of Play

At the end of the tour, after Dean has shown Chris family photographs, ephemera from exotic locations, and has ruminated on the "privilege" of experiencing other cultures, Chris is brought into the kitchen where he is introduced to Georgina (Betty Gabriel), the in-house servant. Cheekily, Dean adds, "My mother loved her kitchen so we keep a piece of her in here." Chris is framed in a close-up as he greets Georgina with a look of curiosity and suspicion. The soft violin and harp chords rising on the soundtrack underscore his growing skepticism around the family's progressiveness Rose had assured him of earlier. On cue, Dean takes Chris out to "the field of play," the expansive property behind the Armitage home where the "nearest house is across the lake." As they walk, Chris makes eye contact for a second time with the groundskeeper. Noticing Chris' expression Dean nudges him and says, "I know what you're thinking. I get it, white family, black servants, it's a total cliché." Chris tells him, "I wasn't going to take it there," to which Dean replies, "Well, you didn't have to." Dean tells Chris that Walter (Marcus Henderson) and Georgina cared for his parents, and that when they passed away rather than letting them go he decided to have them stay and work in a different capacity. Apologizing for "the way it looks," Dean adds: "By the way, I would have voted for Obama a third time."

Parroting Rose's remark to Chris back in his apartment, again the figure of Obama is invoked as a soothing balm at a moment when white liberalism under racial scrutiny seeks a certificate of authenticity in support of its purported aversion to racism. The line also plays like script rehearsed in advance by the Armitage family that leverages Obama's go-for-broke bipartisan politics and the communal sensibility attached to liberal fantasies of "post-race," racial integration, and colorblindness. While on the face of things it plays convincingly like a daughter who knows her father in that way children are uniquely able to identify their parents' habits of speech and patterns of behavior, what we begin to see are the early signs of the scripted artifice of the situation.

Black Bodies

Rose and her parents sit with Chris in a gazebo and go through the motions of getting to know him. The conversation they have is composed in three parts. First, Chris is probed about his parents (the details of which Dean and Missy obviously have foreknowledge). As Chris explains that his father "wasn't really in the picture" (an interesting phrase for a photographer) and that his mother was killed in a hit and run accident, through hypnotic induction Missy links his traumatic recollection to the tapping of a spoon against a glass of iced tea, an action that will later serve as the psychic trigger that paralyzes Chris before he is plunged into the sunken place. Second, Dean notices Chris showing signs of nicotine withdrawal and assures him that Missy could rid him of the habit through hypnosis. Chris politely declines. Finally, Dean tells Rose and Chris that he is happy they are visiting on the weekend of the annual "shindig" started by his father. At this moment, Georgina begins circling the table and refilling the glasses of iced tea. As Dean describes the event and how it began, Georgina appears to lose concentration, staring blankly into the distance, before spilling iced tea on the table. Seeing Georgina's response to Dean speaking about the weekend's events, Missy suggests that she take a break and lie down and Georgina, grinning widely, agrees. What we will soon come to learn is Georgina's episode is not random or anomalous, it is the flicker of a stirring Black consciousness that has been severed from its own body so that a white life can continue flourish.

The conversation ends when Rose's brother, Jeremy (Caleb Landry Jones), arrives. In the following scene Chris is having dinner with Rose and her family. Jeremy, who is clearly inebriated, teases Rose with humiliating stories from her teenaged years. The conversation soon turns to athletics leading Jeremy to ask Chris if he is into mixed martial arts or if he has ever been in a street fight. Jeremy adds, "With your frame and genetic makeup, if you really trained, if you really pushed your body, you would be a fucking beast." Rose and her parents feign embarrassment at Jeremy's remarks, but their concern may have more to do with fear of alerting Chris to the machinations at hand than the social indiscretions of their lubricated son. After grabbing and attempting to wrestle with Chris (who politely declines), Dean and Missy gently admonish Jeremy who says, "I wasn't going to hurt him," before taking a bottle of wine and exiting the room. Taken at face value, Jeremy appears to be assuring his parents that he had only intended to play wrestle with Chris, but what he is really saying to Mom and Dad is that he was not going to harm the merchandise—the Black body—before Chris is introduced to the "party" guests the next day and is auctioned off.

"How are you so calm?"

Later that night as Chris and Rose get ready for bed, Rose animatedly recounts for Chris the interactions he has had to endure since arriving at the Armitage home (as if not already clear to him). Faux-aghast, she puzzles over her mother reprimanding Georgina, and why her brother wanted to put him into a headlock, and "My Dad with this 'my man stuff', now everything is 'my man, my man' I don't think he's ever said that in his life." Rose seems to have forgotten that after their conversation with the police officer and Chris gazing admiringly upon her as they entered the Armitage compound, she also told Chris, "I'm not going to let anyone fuck with my man." While the context may be different, I would argue that the spirit of its use between father and daughter is contiguous. "How are they any different than that cop?" Rose muses as she continues her performance of outrage. Chris softly acknowledges Rose's complaints with non-verbal affirmations, prompting Rose to ask, "Anything more you'd like to add?" To which Chris finally replies, "I told you so."

What a close reading of these four narrative segments linking Chris' departure from his apartment to Rose's bogus outrage reveals is the pervasiveness of microaggressions in quotidian Black life and the careful, practiced strategies Black people are compelled to implement as they move through worlds of white privilege. From the moment Chris motions to comply with the police officer's request for his identification and his attempt to assure Rose he does not mind offering it up for inspection, to his practiced guffaw at Dean asking how long "this *thang*" has been going on, then having to listen to Dean offer explanations for having Black domestic staff in what amounts to the familiar "I'm not a racist" speech white people often make recourse to when their privilege or racism becomes naked and apparent, to Jeremy explaining to Chris what his Black body could be capable of should he apply himself vigorously to physical training. Noting how racism moves through these episodes, Rose, stunned by Chris' composure asks, "How are you so calm?" What Rose fails to realize is that Chris' composure is a skill Black people have had to develop and refine to remain collected in the face of persistent soft racism.

As noted in the previous chapter, microaggressions are often defined as "sudden, stunning, or dispiriting transactions."[20] While it is true that microaggressions are largely comprised of "small acts" of racial ignorance and insensitivity, what Chris experiences is quite the opposite from "sudden, stunning, or dispiriting." In fact, Chris appears to react as if these interactions are common between Black people and white people, and it is the apparent ordinariness of it all that is crucial to the structure of the film's first act.

ROSE: I'm sorry
CHRIS: No, no, no, Come here.
ROSE: I'm sorry, this sucks.

CHRIS: Why are you saying sorry?
ROSE: Because I'm related to them and this sucks.
CHRIS: No, it's fine.
ROSE: Yeah?
CHRIS: Yeah.
ROSE: How are you so calm?
CHRIS: Honestly, it's nothing.

This brief bedside exchange is the full culmination of the day's microaggressions. Though it is entirely appropriate for Chris to tell Rose "I told you so," or to push further and use the day's events as a teachable moment for Rose and illustrate for her that everything he has experienced since leaving his apartment is not anomalous or aberrant, but rather characterizes life in Black America Now, he elects instead to preserve her comfort. It is truly distressing to see Chris become pliant and tell Rose, "It's fine, it's ok … ."

By reassuring Rose and capping off the denial and displacement of his feelings toward being racialized, Chris shows Rose that bracketing away racism is customary to Black people, especially when it comes to preserving white comfort. Rather than come uncoiled from outrage, Chris adopts a forgiving tone. This tone of forgiveness is the net sum of a social pedagogy that maligns "Black anger" or sensitivity to acts not openly perceived as racist or offensive (microaggressions). Chris has obviously been well-schooled in the preservation of white comfort from a lifetime of moving through worlds of white privilege and deflecting racial ignorance. We see these trained forms of preserving white comfort every time a Black person removes the hood on their head so as not to frighten white passers-by, or when they walk a different route away from the lone white person on an empty street, or divert course to avoid a white person sitting alone in a parked car. Though there are more microaggressions to come, this moment is the film's *coup de grace*: "No, it's fine," is the sad, disingenuous mantra of Black life under colorblind neoliberalism.

The Sunken Place

Restless and awake, Chris steps outside the Armitage home in the middle of the night for a cigarette. Strange events abound. Walter appears unexpectedly out of the darkness and runs at Chris in a dead sprint, evading a direct hit only at the last moment. Looking back toward the house, Chris sees Georgina gazing blankly out of a top floor window. A subsequent shot reveals she is actually looking at a translucent reflection of herself as she peers into the window, not through it. When Chris reenters the home, light of foot so as not to wake the family, he finds Missy in the dark waiting for him in her office. She turns the lights on and asks Chris to take a seat across from her. There is an awkward tone to the moment as Missy begins to set the trap put into motion earlier at the gazebo when Chris spoke of the death of his mother. Missy explains how hypnosis works to Chris who, visibly suspicious for he had earlier made it clear he did not wish to be hypnotized for his nicotine habit slips back into the performative mode of preserving white comfort. His gestures, expressions, docile temperament, and even keel tone further extend his pliant disposition through the microaggressions from earlier. Missy begins stirring the teacup with her spoon as she did at the gazebo when asking Chris about his parents. A trap set has now been sprung. By fusing the sound of the spoon against the teacup to Chris' traumatic memory of his mother, Missy has devised an effective method for hypnotic induction that taps into Chris' "heightened suggestibility."

The tone of the conversation shifts abruptly when Missy asks, "What about your mother?" Stunned, Chris pauses momentarily, "Wait, are we … " he says, the façade of the pliant Black man coming undone. "Where were you when she died?" asks Missy, to which Chris replies, "I don't want to think about that." But it is too late. Missy scrapes the spoon against the cup and soon Chris begins speaking the traumatic past, involuntarily opening his psyche to Missy who will pry and splay it wide open by forcing Chris to revisit the moment of his mother's death. Through tears, Chris reluctantly recounts how he became paralyzed with fear after hearing his mother hit by a car in the rain outside of their home. The sequence is meticulously constructed. Peele crosscuts Chris sitting in the chair in Missy's office with an image of Chris as a boy sitting in front of his TV at precisely the moment his mother was struck down. We see young Chris nervously scratching the armrests of his chair; Chris, in the present, is also scratching the armrests of the chair he is sitting in. Peele's compositions begin to tighten as Missy drills deeper into the shattering moment of Chris' early life as the memory of his mother's death and his inaction to potentially intervene on her behalf are brought to the surface.

Missy asks Chris, "how do you feel?" to which Chris replies, "I can't move." In her reply, Missy reveals to Chris the purpose of their interaction and what his entire relationship with Rose has been about: "You're paralyzed." Finally, in what has become an iconic moment in the history of Black American cinema, Missy commands Chris to "sink into the floor." Once she utters this command, as if thrown overboard from the deck of a ship, Chris (both past and present) sinks into darkness where we see him as an adult falling/floating, looking up from a black void toward a distant screen framing what was moments ago his immediate reality. In a hollow echo, we hear Missy tell Chris, "Now you're in the sunken place."

What is the sunken place? What is this black abyss into which Chris sinks and becomes suspended? How has his consciousness been cleaved from his body? Why has his visual field become a distant screen? Why have his screams been silenced? To grasp the full impact of this scene it must be understood as part of a larger process. What Chris will soon come to learn is that while brought to the Armitage home under the pretense of family introductions, he is actually the target of a large-scale white supremacist operation that seduces, coerces, then abducts Black people whose bodies are sold at a private auction. Once a Black body has been purchased, its new owner undergoes a proprietary medical procedure that removes their consciousness from their white body and trans/plants it into the acquired Black body. Before the trans/plantation of white life into Black bodies can be completed, Black consciousness must be set into a state of suspension and the Black body paralyzed. The sunken place names this penultimate stage of the process.

The explicit purpose of the sunken place is to displace Black consciousness from its body to make a clearing for white occupation and control. In the feature-length commentary of *Get Out*, Peele describes the sunken place in pragmatic terms. He notes that in order for the surgical procedure to work, the person on whom it is performed must be conscious. This is the explicit purpose of the sunken place, but it also holds a deep reservoir of implicit meanings. Peele notes that when he wrote the scene it occurred to him that what he was writing about was the prison industrial complex and how Black men end up being trapped and lost in systems of profit-driven incarceration. In her book *The New Jim Crow: Mass Incarceration in the Age of Colorblindness,* Michelle Alexander shows how the prison industrial complex and mass incarceration perpetuates the systematic oppression and subjugation of Black people in America begun in the Middle Passage and chattel slavery. It follows then that if we can think of the sunken place in relation to the prison industrial complex, we can also establish connections to colonialist enterprise and domination that motored transatlantic slavery and the American slave trade through the "birth of a nation" and four centuries of Black enslavement.

The sunken place is the archeo-psychic time of slavery. As Christina Sharpe writes, modernity is marked and defined by "the reappearances of the slave ship in everyday life in the form of the prison, the camp, and the school."[21] To this list, we can add the Black psyche. The sunken place is a rupture in time and space where traumas from the past are conjured into the present to be weaponized. It is a condition of physical arrest where the Black body is rendered immobile so as better to answer the demands issued by a Master. Time passes by on the "screen" of the visible world, but in the archeo-psychic time of the sunken place all is indefinitely suspended. To put it into Sharpe's terms, the sunken place is in and of the wake: "In the wake, the past that is not past reappears, always, to rupture the present."[22] It is, of course, not a coincidence that Sharpe's account of the afterlives of slavery should dovetail easily with Peele's powerful metaphor of Black bodily theft, forced imprisonment, and servitude. As was the Middle Passage, the sunken place is both a locus of irreparable trauma, a site of enduring memory, and a passage into bondage and enslavement, powerfully vivifying slavery and its spectral persistence.

Despite some similarities, there is an important distinction to be made between the phenomenology of transatlantic slavery and the sunken place. Some have argued that the sunken place resembles the hold of a slave ship and that "Chris is in a dark hole where his suffering is unseen and unheard from the 'actors' of modernity steering the ship," but (aside from allusions to the verticality between the deck and hull of the ship) it does not actually resemble, in form or feeling, the hold of a slave ship.[23] The slave ship's hold was a site of collective human dismantling. We must recall that the bondage, pain, trauma and forced labor of the slave ship hull was a shared space with other captives and the affective networks formed under these conditions differs significantly from the abduction techniques devised by the Armitage family, and this difference, I would contend, is strategic. The sunken place was invented to isolate Black people from kinship ties and collective networks.[24] It maliciously leverages individual traumas and activates those deep wells of pain and suffering to snap Black consciousness free from its body. In this iteration of New World slavery, the sunken place begins the process of uprooting Black consciousness from its psychic soil and marks a waypoint along a path toward the depletion of resources used to shore up its stability in worlds of white privilege.

Missy Armitage's potent combination of trauma and hypnosis operates under the pretense of curative intervention, but instead stages an ameliorative promise for purposes of debilitation. She links Chris' smoking habit to childhood trauma and draws out the death of his mother and the guilt he harbors over his inaction in her fatal accident as a tool to take hold of his mind and seize his body. This move is characteristic of the whole clandestine nature of the operation. Here we learn that Black trauma is never bracketed away from white supremacy. It proves time and again to be readily available to be attached to other modes of domination and oppression.

Chris flails wildly as he falls into the dark abyss into which Missy has cast him. What he sees now of the world beyond the sunken place is through a distant screen as if lost in a cinema of his own. The screen, as both frame and camera lens, that has for all of his life functioned as a protective barrier between Chris and the outside world becomes the very site/sight of his oppression. It is remarkable that once cast into the sunken place Chris falls into darkness and looks up at an anamorphic image. While this moment does serve as a powerful metaphor for transatlantic slavery, it evokes the equally powerful metaphor of the cinema and the types of screens Chris has used to refract his trauma.

At the level of form, this moment dramatically closes the bracket opened in the film's beginning. The image of Missy staring at Chris in the sunken place from across a partition marries the parallel image tracks of the Stay Woke sequence and its spatio-temporal separation of Rose and Chris, making explicit in a single shot what was alluded to from the start: Chris is an object of the white gaze. He is something to be looked over, objectively contemplated, abstractly considered, monetized and exchanged; he is, in a word, fungible. A white gaze whose distance and separation the structure of the Stay Woke sequence had maintained now supplants the reflection of his identity previously contained in the frame of the mirror. In a rather brilliant turn, Chris looks at the frame before him and sees not an image of himself in whiteface in his bathroom mirror, in its stead (literally) the white gaze stares back.

Black Specificity

In an essay titled "The Shell Game: From 'Get Out' to 'Parasite,'" Anne Anlin Cheng suggests that Bong Joon-ho's award-winning *Parasite* (2019) and *Get Out* share some key "thematic echoes."[25] As Cheng puts it, "the tropes of spatial and psychical verticality; the theme of ghosts and hauntings; the revelation of intimacy that harbors violence; even elegant garden parties that tend to go awry." While proposing that "We might think of *Parasite* as a South Korean rewrite of *Get Out*," Cheng does caution that the comparison "threatens to elide" important elements unique to the filmic worlds of each, not the least of which is "American racism as a product of the longue durée of American slavery." Finally, Cheng poses the question: "Having your body stolen is surely more traumatic than having your house stolen ... or is it?"[26]

While I certainly do not pretend to have at the ready the kind of social abacus that might make possible calculating for purposes of comparison the literal theft of a Black body into permanent servitude against the symbolic "theft" of a nice home in an upscale neighborhood in South Korea, I will hazard a speculative response to what I can only imagine is a rhetorical question: Yes, having your Black body stolen and auctioned off into New World slavery is the more traumatic of the two. While it is true, as Cheng points out, that issues of race and class are inseparable, the forms of prejudice, alienation, and disenfranchisement each inspires and the veins of oppression they tap into are not identical. This, as Wilderson might call it, is the ruse of analogy. To put it somewhat bluntly and in rather minimalistic terms there is risk involved when folding differing experiences of racial and class oppression into a neat and tidy uniformity on the strength of formal and thematic similarity. The struggles against hegemonic power and marginalization different races or oppressed groups face cannot and should not be fused as one. It follows then that the metaphors that relay experiences of oppression in specific racial or minority groups are not always sharable.

There are stress points in Cheng's use of the sunken place as a conceptual framework for understanding the relationship in *Parasite* between the Kim family and the Park family that need pointing out. In her analysis, Cheng claims, "the 'sunken place' for the Parks is that hidden basement and what lives in it. It is a piece of apt irony that Geun-se was literally the "ghost" that had traumatized the Parks' young son when he was but a toddler and accidentally saw Geun-se as he was creeping out of the basement to steal food from the immaculate kitchen. This 'troubled' child has for many years grown up haunted by this invisible man who is both stranger and housemate." In sum, Cheng's position is that the Park home is a "dream house founded on a sunken place."[27]

I want to push back against this reading and to argue instead for what I am calling here, rather inelegantly, *Black specificity*. The sunken place names a site of subjection that is unique to Black experience. It is a white supremacist invention designed specifically to set Black consciousness into somatic suspension so that the Black body can be seized, auctioned off, and finally made into a host-body for white life, liberty, and the pursuit of happiness. The metaphorical radius of the sunken place is delimited by transatlantic slavery. It is a psychic extension of the prison industrial complex and other carceral continuums where Black life is immobilized and held captive in perpetuity. Moreover, its imaginary power draws on the aquatic symbolism it conjures. Here, again, we can point to Sharpe's various mobilizations of the term "wake" in the context of the afterlife of slavery. When Sharpe speaks of the wake, she recalls that Black bodies were often flung dead or almost dead into the wake of passing slave ships along the ocean's surface to sink and perish into its depths.

We might also recall the closing moments of *Black Panther* (2018) when Killmonger tells T'Challa, who offers to save his life after striking him with a mortal wound, "Throw me into the ocean with my ancestors who knew that death was better than bondage." These aquatic linkages of sinking and slavery are the undertow of its symbolic force. What we also learn about the sunken place is that it is a visual field—a panoptic zone—where Black bodies are snared in vectors of the white gaze, it is a zone where Black screams are silenced, and Black subjectivity is decentered and paralyzed. In sum, the sunken place is a zone unique to Black oppression under white supremacy and any attempts to deploy it in other racial contexts elide its operative design and constitutive symbolism.

Returning to Wilderson, whose observations in another context aptly respond to Cheng's line of inquiry:

> To face the realization that one is a worker and not a capitalist is far less traumatic than the realization that one is a Black, a Slave, and not a Human. The former revelation is not nearly as traumatic as one in which the sentient being wakes up to find that she has no capacities for Human production; and, furthermore, comes to understand that just as economic production is parasitic on the labor power of the working class, the production of Human capacity is parasitic on the flesh of the Slave, the Black.[28]

The Sunken Place in Popular Culture

In the ensuing years since the film's release the sunken place has developed into a term describing a special disconnect between Black identity and the brutal history that has shaped, and continues to shape, life in Black America Now. Public figures like Ben Carson, Tiger Woods, Sage Steele and Kanye West have all in one way or another disavowed the idea that to be Black in America is to occupy a position of structural disadvantage.

The episodes of reverse racial dysmorphia associated with these individuals have been well documented and hardly need rehearsing, but a sampling of headlines from Black popular culture online magazine *TheRoot.com* brings the matter into sharper focus. In an April 12, 2017, article covering the Trump administration's Housing and Urban Development Secretary Ben Carson's visit to an affordable housing complex in Miami, Florida, author Stephen A. Crockett Jr. makes light of an incident in which Carson and others were briefly trapped inside of the building's elevator. The title of the article reads, "Ben Carson Visits Miami Public Housing and Gets Trapped in 'the Sunken Place.'" In an article from Jay Connor on December 23, 2019, the title reads, "Ben Carson Emerges from The Sunken Place to Opine on Reparations … ." Another article from August 25, 2017, on sports news anchor Sage Steele, a vocal advocate for keeping race politics out of sports broadcasting, is titled "Why Sage Steele Needs to Go Sit Down and Stare Longingly at the Stirring Teaspoon." And in response to the napalm tweeting of Kanye West another headline reads, "The Sunken Place Has Good Wi-Fi, so Now We Have (Not So) Deep Tweets by Kanye West." As recently as March 11, 2021, *TheRoot.com* published an article hilariously titled "Stacey Dash Denounces Trump and Fox News and Is Now Sunken Place-Free. Well, Not Really, but Kind of … Man, Just Read." But if there is one example of the sunken place being used in its vernacular sense that stands out among the rest, it comes from Jordan Peele himself who after seeing Tiger Woods photographed golfing with then President Donald Trump in November of 2017 retweeted an image of Woods and Trump shaking hands with the caption "Now you're in The Sunken Place."

While this usage differs from the definition Peele offers in his feature-length commentary for the film's home release, it speaks to how the phrase has become shorthand for a condition where selective amnesia undergirds racial delusion. Again, credit must be given to Peele for the timeliness of the sunken place as a concept that elucidates a small but persistent facet of Black experience in contemporary neoliberal society. As Tananarive Due points out, the sunken place has become "a conceptual glyph that explains Black people who support Donald Trump, the NFL's collusion to keep Colin Kaepernick out of football for kneeling to protest police brutality, the death of Sandra Bland after an illegal traffic stop, and a nation with roots in slavery that stubbornly refuses to own up to that legacy and the white supremacy that survived emancipation."[29]

There are several common factors shared across the photograph of Woods with Trump, then West with Trump on several different occasions culminating with West openly wearing a MAGA (Make America Great Again) hat, and the examples of Sage Steele and Ben Carson. They seem to suggest it is possible to be Black in America while being unyoked from the semiotics of Blackness or that it is possible to either compartmentalize historical events or that the collective traumas of the past should remain in the past and if left undisturbed the path to racial reconciliation will be smoothly paved. To prop up this delusion, recourse is often made to their own personal lives as the preferred method for gauging anti-Black discrimination. Take as an example political commentator Kmele Foster who in an appearance on HBO's *Real Time with Bill Maher* on January 22, 2021, went on to make numerous untenable claims about racial inequality in America and its impact on the Black community. Arguably the most narrow-sighted among them that "Anyone who looks at me and sees someone disadvantaged is sorely mistaken," a comment that was received by Maher and his (presumably) mostly white audience with cheers of affirmation. The episode's co-panelist Peter Hamby seemed thunderstruck, in the most composed sense of the word, by the curious omission of reality from Foster's worldview with Maher at one point going so far as to decry "critical race theory" by name. The spectacle of Foster tangled inside a web of racial delusion of his own spinning exemplifies perfectly the vernacular sense of what it means to be trapped in the sunken place.

This is what makes these public Black figures compelling puppets for post-racial ideology who parrot talking points around the fantasy of an equal opportunity America. You will often hear that it is only the persistent focus on historical traumas that stokes the fires of racial grievance, and if Black people would concern themselves less with the past, racism would vanish like a rabbit from a magician's top hat. It is not at all surprising that Missy Armitage should have to traffic in the on and off ramps of memory and trauma to induce the sinking of Black consciousness into the sunken place; racial amnesia seems to be its precondition (or its passcode). Just as Chris is not able to recollect in full what occurred during his forced hypnosis and cannot recollect (and therefore recognize) that his consciousness has been cleared away to make space for white life to install its habits of thought and speech into his body, so too is it the case that West, Carson, Steele, Woods, Foster, and so many more seem to have had traumatic memory (be it personal or collective) debrided, cauterized and wiped clean so that the tenets of neoliberal white post-racial thinking can be invisibly sutured into place.

Strategies of the Microaggressed

With the psychic trapdoor of the sunken place set, Chris is ready to be auctioned off. The next day a fleet of black vehicles arrive at the Armitage estate and Rose shepherds Chris through rounds of introductions with guests who, unbeknownst to him, are actually bidders participating in an auction for his body. The microaggressions from the previous day continue. Rose introduces Chris to three elderly white couples and the conversations play out as follows: In the first introduction, Chris is complimented on the grip of his handshake and asked if he plays golf. "Once a few years ago, but I wasn't very good," he replies. After telling Chris he knows Tiger Woods, the man sets up into a golf swing stance and says, "So, Chris, let's see your form."

In the next introduction another elderly white couple fawns over Chris' body. This time, a woman approaches Chris and without consent begins rubbing his chest and squeezing his arms. She turns to her husband who is in a wheelchair with an oxygen tube, "Not bad, eh, Neilson?" Finally, she asks Rose, "So, is it true? Is it better?" In the third conversation an elderly white man proclaims, "Black (skin) is in fashion!" Chris, weary from the burden of being polite, excuses himself to take photographs. Here Chris' camera doubles as a barrier between him and the world of white privilege around him. He scans the party through the camera viewfinder, but Dean, surrounded by a half dozen guests, points toward Chris as they all turn in his direction to stare (a synchronized gesture that will be repeated later when Chris walks past the party guests in the house to go upstairs). Even the protective barrier of his camera cannot shield him from the objectifying power of the white gaze.

In each of these episodes Chris' Blackness is foregrounded (again). The tone of these exchanges range from subtle insinuation ("I know Tiger Woods … " "I would have voted for Obama a third time") to direct reference ("With your body type … " "Is it better?"), and each time Chris' response is practiced in its level headedness, measured tone, and finesse—one might even say it is Obama-like. What we are repeatedly made aware of are the ways Chris responds to racial microaggressions at a bodily level. For every moment Chris' Blackness or Black being in general becomes the focal point of the conversation, he has a facial expression ready to deflect harm, or a posture meant to signal that he is in on the joke. These episodes also lend evidence to Yancy's assertion that "The history of whiteness demonstrates that curious white hands can lead to violent acts of objectifying and experimenting on Black bodies; and desirous white hands can lead to violent and unspeakable acts of molestation, where the Black body undergoes tremendous pain and trauma."[30]

In Cheng's estimation, Chris "failed to read the signs (an off joke here and there, a sight that does not compute) screaming all around him to *get out* the moment he entered the Armitage estate, not because he's blind or deaf to them but because, at some level, he's only all too aware of them." Here I would argue that Chris does not repeatedly fail to read the signs around him, but rather—to Cheng's later point—because he is all too aware of them, he has already primed himself to accept the fact that his Blackness will eventually become a point of focus. He has learned well the social skill all Black folk who must live in and navigate worlds of white privilege learn in order to preserve the façade of pliancy and social grace. On this point Cheng rightly observes that,

> The imperative to get over these moments comes from a place much deeper than regard for social niceties; it arises as a claustrophobic survival instinct. It is about the socially and hence self-imposed injunction to carry on despite the tear in the social fabric, an erupting phantom, a gaping void that you must sidestep ... or be confronted by the utter rejection of your very being by the people smiling around you.[31]

The argument that Chris believes he is in "a narrative of post-Blackness" or that he is an embodiment of post-Blackness ignores the patient, practiced effort Chris must expend in the face of a long chain of microaggressions and overt fetishizations of his Black body.[32] If we understand post-Blackness as being relative to "post-racial," then for one to be in a state of "post-Blackness" would require that one disavow their Blackness as marked "other." In the logics of post-race the playing field is level, all opportunities are equal, the color of one's skin is neither impediment nor advantage, social and professional advancement is meritocratic, staking claim to past grievances are counterproductive, historical amnesia wins the day. Chris, at every turn, is made to face his Blackness. So, in order to navigate this weekend at the home of his white girlfriend, whom he loves and cherishes, he is left with little choice but to meet the incessant focus on the color of his skin with humor and patience.

Chris' introduction to Jim Hudson (Stephen Root), the blind art dealer, offers a compelling and narratively strategic counterbalance to these microaggressions. Chris meets Jim away from the other guests and, as Chris approaches, he declaims: "Ignorance; all of them. They mean well, but have no idea what real people go through." This statement could double as the siren call for counterfeit white wokeness. Peele cleverly designs the Hudson character as a fake white ally proffering the familiar empty jargon of solidarity, woke one-liners, and playacted racial awareness. Jim, a middle-aged white man, in both speech and attitude implies that he is not like the rest of the wealthy white people at the Armitage party. He introduces himself to Chris telling him he admires his photography ("So brutal. So melancholic; I think.") and that he too was once a photographer before becoming an art dealer. As he tells it to Chris, "I used to dabble myself, wilderness mostly. Submitted to NatGeo (National Geographic) fourteen times before realizing I didn't have the eye."

Jim's story of failure and disappointment is apiece with the story of father Armitage's failure after losing to Jesse Owens in the Berlin Olympics. And so another white man haunted by failure and disappointment with money to burn sees the Black body and the radical possibility of inhabiting it as a solution to acquiring abilities he does not inherently possess. In worlds of white privilege, the guiding principle is if you can't beat them, become them; what you don't have, you can always acquire: life, liberty, and the pursuit of happiness are yours for the taking. The destiny of the Black body in America has always toggled between sites of white fear and white becoming. Already seated in the chair from which he will place his bid to win the auction, Chris tells Jim, "Shit ain't fair," to which Jim replies loaded and flatly, "You're right, shit ain't fair."

Black Fraternity and Recognition

There are two moments in the film that raise the issue of Black fraternity. First, Chris spots another Black man at the party standing by the refreshments table. He lowers his camera—as if to signal he is lowering his guard—and approaches the man whose back is turned to him. Peele holds Chris in a medium shot center frame for a moment as his expression turns from puzzlement to pleasant surprise. As Chris approaches the other man his posture and demeanor begin to change. With an expression that can only be described as relief, Chris taps the man on the arm from behind and says, "Good to see another brother around here."

In *So You Want to Talk About Race*, Ijeoma Oluo describes the experience of Black recognition as that moment of unexpectedly encountering another Black person and sharing a moment of mutual acknowledgment. It is, as Oluo puts it, that moment when Black strangers signal to each other, "I see you fam."[33] Peele captures the spirit of these coded encounters of recognition and unspoken fraternity in detail in order to overturn them for dramatic effect. The visible shift in Chris' demeanor and expression, the familiar tap on the man's arm, and the admission that it's nice to see "another brother" are all signs of Black fraternity, but when the "other brother" turns to face Chris, those signals become crossed. As it turns out, the other Black man at the party is Andre, the man strangled and abducted in the film's opening sequence. Chris, of course, is not aware of this, but immediately intuits something is amiss.

The man replies, "Ah, yes, of course it is." Chris' expression of relief turns to suspicion. The man introduces himself not as Andre, but as Logan King before leaning in and saying to his white wife who has now joined them, "Chris was just telling me how he felt much more comfortable with my being here." The code of Black fraternity in a white space is here betrayed, but what makes this encounter all the more uncanny is that while this fraternal code is tacitly known, it is not meant to be acknowledged. To repeat Chris' admission that he is more comfortable with another Black person around to a white person is an explicit breach of this unspoken fraternal contract. As if to make certain the peculiarity of this moment is not a misunderstanding, when Logan and his wife motion to leave, Chris extends his fist to give Logan pound, but Logan reciprocates with an open palm. It is one of the film's more memorable images, one used prominently in advertising campaigns and marketing materials because its power lies in the surety of Black fraternal bonds signified in giving pound or a familiar handshake. Peele knows this failure of fraternal recognition between Black people is so potent a visual cue that something is off, he frames the miscued handshake in close-up.

The second occasion of failed Black fraternity occurs not long after the introduction to Logan. Chris returns to his bedroom and finds that his phone has been unplugged. Suspecting Georgina may have intentionally unplugged it, Chris shares his suspicions with Rose who, again, responds dismissively with humor to lull Chris into thinking the accusation is absurd. Naturally, Chris' suspicions are correct, and at this point in the narrative—after walking through a room of white people who were pretending to engage in small talk, but who, unbeknownst to Chris, fall silent and watch him intently as he walks upstairs to the bedroom—it is certain that Chris is in peril. He deploys his familiar "It's fine, it's fine," response to Rose. But moments later, after an amusing phone call between Chris and Rod, Georgina enters the bedroom to apologize for unplugging the phone. Near the end of their conversation they share the following exchange:

CHRIS: It's fine. I wasn't trying to snitch.
GEORGINA: Snitch?
CHRIS: Rat you out.
GEORGINA (CONFUSED): Tattle tale?
CHRIS: (BEGRUDGINGLY): Yeah

Chris' failure to connect with the other Black people at the Armitage residence through Black vernacular and social habitus marks the missing passcodes in these interactions. The counterpoint to these short-circuited episodes of Black fraternity is Dean parroting the phrases "my man" and "this thang" in a playacted attempt at deploying Black vernacular to make him feel at ease.

Get Out!

At the third and final round of introductions, Chris can now barely contain his frustrations. A guest (notably, an Asian man and the only non-white guest at the party) asks Chris, "Do you find being African-American is more advantage or disadvantage in the modern world?" Nonplussed, Chris spots Logan King near the group and deflects the question his way: "They want to know about the African-American experience. Why don't you take this one." Replying earnestly, Logan admits, "I find that the African-American experience has been, for me, for the most part very good." Stunned by the response, Chris covertly takes a picture of Logan with his phone, but the flash goes off unexpectedly. Logan pauses. Blood runs from his nose. The white light of the camera flash pools in his irises as his expression contorts into fear and panic. Momentarily freed from the sunken place it is Andre not Logan who lunges at Chris, balling up his shirtfront in his fists yelling, "Get out! Get out!!" Here it is not the mirror, but flash photography which in its duplicative process stuns the invading white parasite long enough to make a clearing for Andre's consciousness to return and declare its pleas for freedom. It is not only Chris to whom the utterance "Get out!" is being spoken, that demand is also being made by Andre to the white invader colonizing his Black body.

This moment is both narratively and conceptually a median point between what we know about the sunken place after seeing Chris plunged into its depths against his will and what we will soon come to learn about the broader stratagem of abduction unfolding. In the following scene, Dean (with a brilliant play on "seizure") offers Chris and the guests an explanation: "Seizures can cause anxiety which can trigger aggression." Dean and Missy cleverly attempt to simultaneously paper the cracks and explain away both

Logan's eruption to Chris and the potential flaw in the Coagula process to its investors soon to bid on his body. But Chris, moments later, makes it clear to Rose as they sit by a nearby lake that he does not believe what occurred was the result of a seizure (at least in the sense he believes Dean is using the term). Even though Rose attempts to placate his suspicions by reminding Chris that her dad is a neurosurgeon, he knows something is not right and he expresses to her a sense of familiarity not with Logan, but more remarkably with the *Black body* that accosted him. What is important to note here is how Chris' response continues a pattern of inaction against his intuition and common sense despite the fact it is becoming increasingly apparent to him (and the audience) that he needs to "Get out!"

In his 1983 stand-up comedy show *Delirious*, Eddie Murphy mocks the divergent responses between white and Black characters to hauntings and supernatural threats in horror films. After a screening of *Poltergeist* (1982), Murphy wonders, "Why don't white people just leave the house when there's a ghost in the house?" As Murphy explains it to his audience, "It's very simple: there's a ghost in the house, get the fuck out of the house." He continues, "In *The Amityville Horror* (1977) the ghost told them to get out the house, white people stayed in there." Murphy imagines himself in the house of *The Amityville Horror* with his wife admiring its interior design and the kids playing outside: "I really like it here, this is really nice." Playing the ghost, Murphy whispers, "GET OUT!" then adds, "Too bad we can't stay, baby."

Coincidentally, or perhaps in direct reference to Murphy's bit, Lamberto Bava's 1985 film *Demons* has a Black man (playing a caricature of Black masculinity in American Blaxploitation cinema) accompanied by two Black women arriving at a theater in Berlin for the screening of a zombie film. When one of the women attending the screening with him turns into a demon, and the theatergoers suspect that the projected film may be the cause, the Black man yells for all in the theater to hear: "Get out! Everybody get away! Get out! What are you waitin' for? Run!" Bearing out precisely Murphy's comedic take on white response to horror movie hauntings, we see Black common sense in action. More than the trope of dying first, being able to assess risk in potentially life or death situations and using common sense in the face of danger stands out as the definitive trait Black characters exhibit in horror films.

While both Murphy and the Wayans Brothers highlight Black common sense for comedic effect, I want to suggest that this inherent skepticism and heightened sensitivity to scenarios that could prove threatening has a real world correlate. Being able to recognize, assess, and respond to seemingly innocuous events (particularly in worlds of white privilege) that are, in fact, imperiling is endemic to Black life in America. Like the protocols of "the talk" in *The Hate You Give*, Black people must remain vigilant and stay woke if they hope to survive in Black America Now. It is this epistemology that serves as the reservoir from which Black characters in horror films draw their skepticism and alertness to potential dangers. Reiterating Sharpe's observations on the afterlife of slavery proves instructive here: "Living in the wake means living the history and present of terror, from slavery to the present, as the ground of our everyday Black existence; living the historically and geographically dis/continuous but always present and endlessly reinvigorated brutality in, and on, our bodies while even as terror is visited on our bodies the realities of that terror are erased."[34] Black intuition in horror films cannot be thought apart from this embodiment of terror on Black bodies. And while it is played for humor, it is in fact bound up with traumas that ripple across Black being. But why, then, does Chris, despite this ability to correctly recognize and assess threat, contradict the generic stereotype offered in Murphy's observations?

Powers of Intuition

Black characters in horror films possess sharper faculties of common sense than their white counterparts. In horror film after horror film we see Black characters who are preternaturally aware of impending danger trying to convince white people to "wake up" or "get out!" and run for their lives. When white characters do exhibit the gift of foresight, they are often physically blind. *Get Out* plays with this trope in three separate, but interlocking scenarios. First, Andre is walking through a suburban neighborhood and immediately intuits jeopardy despite the fact there is nothing immediately, or identifiably, threatening. That is, until the white Porsche arrives. True to Black character typology, Andre senses danger, correctly identifies it when it becomes apparent, but (an important "but") still falls victim to the threat as he tries to act on behalf of his own survival.

In the second scenario, Rod jokingly reminds Chris of the potential danger he is putting himself in by traveling to the suburbs to visit Rose's family. As events at the Armitage estate unfold and Chris shares with Rod some of the strange incidents that have occurred, he implores Chris to cut his visit short and return to the city immediately. The comedic tone of Rod's warnings and intuitions are in line with the standard generic responses of Black characters in horror movies. This point is worth emphasizing because horror films tend to deploy the preternatural intuitions of Black characters or, at the very least, their heightened facility for common sense as moments of comedic relief within the economy of modern horror narratives (the entire *Scary Movie* franchise is predicated on this). These clarion calls of Black survival are rarely if ever taken seriously and typically function as little more than speed bumps along the route to the inevitable dismissal of Black characters from the film.

This is frequently the case in white story arcs (the horror genre's predominant form) where white protagonists are the only legitimate contenders for survival against the monster(s) that seek to eliminate them. Rod asks, "How are you not scared of this, bruh?" The moment plays for comedic effect, as Rod's role in the film is to proffer levity and provide the humor necessary to balance the gravity of the story. Chris' response to Rod, on one hand, calls into question his status as a woke

Black character, and there are reasons (like strategies of the microaggressed) to explain away the signs Rod tries to call to Chris' attention, but there is one reason in particular that seems most compelling.

Back at the lake where Chris tries to convince Rose that the Logan/Andre episode was not a seizure, where he admits to her that since the forced hypnotism by her mother he has been thinking "all this fucked up shit that I don't want to think about," where he will eventually confess to Rose that on the morning of his mother's death, as he sat transfixed in the glow of a television screen, his mother lay dying (not dead) in the street "cold and alone." This is the film's pivotal moment, the centrifuge around which all preceding narrative events spin into revelation. Chris says to Rose, "You're all I got. I'm not going to leave here without you, I'm not going to abandon you." And there, in a single statement, his face naked and earnest, Chris brings into view the horizon against which all of the day's microaggressions have been allowed to pass, the essence of his grace and finesse in his dealings with Rose's family and the party guests (Black and white); in a single statement he answers all of the questions asked of him: "How are you so calm?" "How are you not scared of this, bruh?"

Some critics have suggested that if Chris is woke he should be capable of recognizing that he is in a horror movie narrative, and that all of the microaggressions and subtle racist remarks he has had to endure lend evidence to forms of Black social marginalization he should be aware of and actively contest.[35] Alternatively, I argue that Chris, in fact, clearly recognizes the situation he is in. Chris does not read the signs the way Rod interprets them not because he lacks the intuition or common sense that Rod possesses, qualities conventional to Black characters in horror films, but because he does not *want* to see the signs as such. To recognize the signs as they appear to him, all of which signal that he is in a situation he should extricate himself from, is also to enter into the admission that he does not belong in Rose's world. Chris had already expressed this feeling to Rose back in his apartment with the question,

"Do they know I'm black?" before being ushered unawares to the property on which he is scheduled to be auctioned. Stated in the affirmative, another way of expressing the undercurrent of this feeling would be to confess, "I don't belong in your world, but I hope to." This sentiment is common in Hollywood melodramas where class difference operates as an impediment to the union of the heterosexual couple. For example, in *Good Will Hunting* (1997), Skylar asks Will to join her in California, and after a brief disagreement Will's response accelerates quickly into emotional eruption culminating in what amounts to the admission: "I don't belong in your world!" Statements of this kind are rarely heard in race films. The reason for this might have something to do with the ontological magnitude of what is implied. For Black characters in a Hollywood film to admit, "I do not belong in your world," is also to declare that they do not belong to any world at all. Will Hunting can express this feeling for even in the context of an enormous class division, he still remains squarely positioned in a world of white privilege. No such luck for Chris.

Contrary to the evidence before him, Chris hopes that he will be accepted and that everything that he already knows about the dramas of Black and white in America that are contained in the question "Do they know I'm black?" will be bracketed away into exception. This is what makes Chris' story so profoundly sad, for it is his trauma that guides his thinking and his decision-making. His is a life world of melancholy and abandonment, of deep forgotten wells of guilt and regret; it suffuses even his photographs: "so brutal, so melancholic," says Jim, the art dealer. Put plainly, there is no precedent for a character like Chris in the history of American horror films. Chris plays against Black character typology not out of ignorance or a banal reversal of generic codes. Chris is clearly aware that things around him are not adding up: his cell phone is unplugged and left uncharged; he is hypnotized against his will, but wakes up skeptical if it is a dream or reality; the Black groundskeepers behave oddly; a Black guest at the Armitage party who looks familiar to Chris erupts into pleas for Chris to "Get out!" Yet, he knowingly and willingly pushes these incidents aside and proceeds through the film's story arc.

This sets up the devastating conditions of the third episode. Later that evening Chris text messages the picture he took of Andre/Logan to Rod who recognizes him immediately as a missing person from several months earlier. Once Rod recognizes him, Chris also remembers who he is but insists that he seems different, and that he was at the party with a white woman thirty years older than him. Rod yells: "Sex slave! Chris, you gotta get the fuck up outta there!" At this moment the battery on Chris' phone dies and the call is cut short. The "joke" is that Rod is exactly right. Andre has been rendered, quite literally, a sex slave, perpetuating one of the more brutal dimensions of antebellum slavery when enslaved women were raped by their masters.

In his analysis of an episode of the television series *Homeland* (2011–20), Wilderson describes how a CIA operative named Carrie Mathison (a white woman) seduces the nephew of an Afghan Taliban leader as part of a government plot to assassinate his uncle. Carrie and the nephew engage in sexual relations over a three-day period while waiting for his uncle to arrive, but where the nephew believes that the sex is spontaneous and the attraction mutual it is merely a product of carefully orchestrated state machinations. Wilderson shrewdly observes that the scene raises the issue of mutual consent:

> In other words, he does not know he is being raped ... repeatedly raped ... that his consent to this sex has been abrogated by the very structure of the conditions in which the sex takes place. It is a rape scenario because the sex that he mistakes for mutual attraction is really a series of multiple acts of aggression in which his consent has been eviscerated completely.[36]

By emphasizing that the Afghan boy's consent to sexual relations with Carrie is founded on deception, what is also made apparent is his structural vulnerability to her. In other words, immanent to the ontology of her whiteness is a capacity for anti-Black violence that is always available to her and can be weaponized at will (CF: Amy Cooper). Against this background we can see Rod's running joke of sex slavery is anything but a laughing matter. Sex slavery is another name for rape in perpetuity. Like the Afghan boy in *Homeland*, Chris believes his sexual relationship with Rose is consensual, but he has been repeatedly raped from the very beginning through acts of aggression that will eventually leverage his structural vulnerability to her and her whiteness.

Certain now that nefariousness is afoot in the Armitage home, Chris turns to Rose and in a panicked whisper tells her they have to leave the house immediately. She exits the room to get dressed and as Chris is packing his bag he notices an open door to a crawl space. Again, in flagrant defiance of Black character typology, rather than running from the house immediately, he stops to look inside (what amounts to the horror genre's standard ill-advised excursion into the basement, or the attic, or the woods outside) where he discovers a shoebox filled with pictures of Rose with a dozen other Black partners, Walter and Georgina included. The scale of the treachery comes into view. As he puts the shoebox full of photos back where he found them, Rose reenters the room and asks if he is ok, to which Chris simply asks for the keys to the car. In one final performative deception, Rose looks for the keys in her bag, but tells Chris she cannot find them. As they walk downstairs to leave, Dean, Missy and Jeremy are waiting for them. Chris knows very well that he will not be getting keys from Rose despite her playacted search through her bag. What this final example of the intuitive Black character illustrates is that in spite of knowing very well that his life is imperiled and that he should act swiftly and immediately to secure his survival, he elects instead to ignore what his rational deductions and senses alert him to and chooses the course of wishful thinking.

This same propensity for inaction is bound up with the traumatic episode from Chris' childhood when Chris heard the hit and run outside of the house that killed his mother and he chose wishful thinking and inaction rather than confronting the reality of the situation as he had rightly intuited. Chris' failure to act on those capacities for common sense, intuition, and threat recognition reveal a deep paradox at the center of Black character typology in horror films. While it is true that Black characters frequently are able to recognize threats and the conditions of bodily peril they are in, they are almost never able to capitalize on this ability to the ends of their own survival. At best, this skill serves two predominant functions: First, to aid in the survival of the white characters who lack this skill but directly benefit from it, which rather spectacularly reinforces the cultural superstructures of white supremacy's theft of Black ability; and the second, to provide comic relief and facilitate the periods of relaxation necessary for the efficacy of the genre's episodic "numbers" of violence and intensity during confrontations between monster and victims.

This paradox signals, I think, a deep-seated logic by which Black intuition surrenders its deductions to the promise—one it is all too aware—worlds of white privilege hold out to white inhabitants. This is the horror film's version of the familiar rhetorical formulation, "I know very well, but … ." One of the assurances held forth by a white world to white inhabitants is that ontological integrity is a birthright and even when safety and security seem imperiled, in the end, (to quote Bob Marley, a beloved and well-trafficked white conduit into Black culture) "everything's gonna be alright."[37] We might recall here the description of white privilege offered earlier: privilege is most effective when it does not recognize itself as privilege. Because it is incapable of full self-reflection it proves inadequate to intervene in the forms of impudence it propagates. White privilege reinforces inherent presumptions of infallibility that ultimately jeopardizes white characters in horror films: Of course going into the basement is fine, why wouldn't it be? (*The Evil Dead*) Of course going upstairs is fine, why wouldn't it be? (*Black Christmas*) Of course going into the woods is fine, why wouldn't it be? (*The Blair Witch Project*) Of course being white and going into a besieged, predominantly Black urban neighborhood is fine, why wouldn't it be? (*Candyman*) This list could continue *ad infinitum*.

One of the most powerful rouses of living Black life in a neoliberal white world is that it is possible for Black existence to safely operate under the same fantasmatic protections that shield white characters endowed with privilege. The long modernity of the American horror film capitalizes on these protections in spaces like the family home, the summer camp, on camping expeditions, cave explorations, backpacking trips in foreign countries (an extension of the power of white privilege to transform other spaces and geographies into zones of whiteness), diving expeditions and other areas and activities populated by the leisure class. Because white characters see these spaces as inherently safe spaces, when they are threatened by the "Other" or become sites of annihilation and undoing, the sense of violation is all the more immense. The paradox, therefore, is that while Black characters in horror films invariably fall somewhere on the intuitional spectrum between divine foresight and common sense and can, as it were, read the writing on the wall and identify the potential threats endangering them and those around them, they function only as oracles for white protagonists or prove powerless in capitalizing on their own intuitive and epistemological advantages.

This is what makes Chris' abduction all the more tragic. Chris, against every impulse and in flagrant denial of Rod's warnings (and his own intuitions), *wants* to believe that he is mistaken. Chris *wants* to believe Rose wants him and that every microaggression he experiences, every act of muted racism, all the moments when his Blackness or his Black body and its potential are foregrounded at the expense of his subjectivity are all reducible to simply how it is and what it means to move through a white world that has fundamentally marked him as other. There is an argument to be made that of all the Black characters in the whole history of American horror films, Chris was provided with more cues to the danger he was in and more signals alerting him to that danger than any other Black character in any horror film before him. To wit: Andre literally grabs Chris and screams "GET OUT!" But, moments later, we find Chris sitting in a room full of white people as Logan, having pushed Andre back into the sunken place with the aid of Missy, explains away the incident.

It should not be forgotten that the Black people in the photographs with Rose are all now Black bodies possessed by a parasitic white consciousness. We can see here why the sunken place functions so effectively as a metaphor for Black people who present as unaware or ignorant of the social and political reality of oppositional struggle in America. One might expect to find in the bottom of Rose's box of photographs pictures of her cuddled up next to Kanye West, Ben Carson, or Sage Steele.

Behold the Coagula

It is no coincidence that the auction for Chris takes the form of a game. As Hartman has eloquently noted, where Blackness in the white imaginary is concerned, pleasure and possession are always intimately linked. While seated on what Dean earlier referred to as the "field of play," participants hold bingo cards like bidding paddles as they vie for Chris' body, and while bingo suggests a game of chance the outcome has already been decided. Each of the bidders holds up a winning card with a single row fully pockmarked by colored marker. As if to reinforce through symbolism the earlier remark made by Chris to Jim and Jim back to Chris that "shit ain't fair," it would seem that the fix is already in. While only one bidder will come away with possession of Chris' body (Jim, no less, still seated where only moments ago he said of the very people around him, "They mean well, but have no idea what real people go through") they all have already been declared winners in the worlds of white privilege they inhabit. From Jim, the "woke" art dealer capping on the other white people at the party, to the *pièce de résistance* (to borrow a term from

Dean) of Rose's master class in deception when she pulls the keys Chris wants so desperately from her bag and flips from hysterical to calm and says, "You know I can't give you the keys, right, babe?" In the film, white allyship is a rouse, which seems in accordance with the standard liberal expressions of "pro-Black" allyship from blacked out boxes in social media feeds to retweets of James Baldwin quotes. As the film makes clear, the ones who appear most well-meaning are often the ones to be most wary of.

The jig is up. Chris will have to fight his way out of the Armitage home if he hopes to escape, but Missy taps the spoon against her teacup and casts him back into the sunken place. Now paralyzed and unconscious, the Armitage clan drag Chris into the basement. When Chris regains consciousness, he finds himself in the family game room. The mise-en-scène reinforces Chris' objectification through the position he occupies among other games: we see shots of a table tennis set, to the left of Chris there is a foosball table and to his right a dartboard and bocce balls. These shots underscore Chris' status as merely one of the available objects of amusement in the room. They not only situate Chris amidst games of leisure reinforcing one of the key tropes of the torture porn film noted earlier, but there is also a sense of recognition from Chris that he is aware that he has been reduced to and conflated with the diversions around him. The game room and Chris' position in the center of the room casts new light on what was alluded to before when Dean introduced Chris to the "field of play," and when Chris and Jim Hudson were speaking while a game of badminton was being played in the background, and, again, to say nothing of the fact that bidders attending the auction for Black bodies place bids by raising bingo cards.

As Chris struggles to free himself from the restraints binding him to a chair (echoing the scene of his traumatic break on the night of his mother's death), the television in front of him turns on. The name of the video introducing the proprietary medical procedure developed by the Armitage family is "*Behold the Coagula.*" This appears to be a reference to a pivotal moment from Ralph Ellison's masterpiece of American fiction *Invisible Man*. Near the end of the novel, the narrator puts on a pair of heavily tinted green glasses and a white hat and is mistaken for a man by the name Rinehart. At first the narrator takes pleasure in having his identity mistaken (there are people looking for him), but soon finds himself trying to convince those who think he is Rinehart that he, in fact, is not. As the narrator walks through the neighborhood he sees a neon sign that reads "HOLY WAY STATION. BEHOLD THE LIVING GOD." Two children approach the narrator and hand him a waybill. On the waybill is a quote from one Rev. B. P. Rinehart that reads,

Behold the Invisible
Thy will be done O Lord
I See all, Know all, Tell all, Cure all.
You shall see the unknown wonders.

The waybill concludes with:

BEHOLD THE SEEN UNSEEN
BEHOLD THE INVISIBLE

The narrator experiences a kind of vertigo as he contemplates how he can inhabit an entirely different identity by donning only a few fashion accoutrements. When someone he believes should recognize him does not, the narrator speculates if his acquaintance is "someone else disguised to confuse me."[38] The narrator soon comes across a waybill with a printed quote from the man with whom he has been confused. It says, "Behold the Seen Unseen. Behold the Invisible." He wonders, "What on earth was hiding behind the face of things? If dark glasses and a white hat could blot out my identity so quickly, who actually was who?"

That the Armitage family business would announce the discovery of a process that permits white identity to colonize Black bodies and swap in new identities with "*Behold the*

Coagula" seems a pointed nod to this moment in Ellison's novel when the protagonist becomes the "seen unseen." And while the declaration "behold the invisible" denotes the mystery and power of the Divine, the phrase more potently carries racial overtones. The narrator, who in the opening sentence of the novel states, "I am an invisible man. No, I am not a spook like those who haunted Edgar Allen Poe; nor am I one of your Hollywood-movie ectoplasms. I am a man of substance and flesh and bone, fiber and liquids—and I might even be said to possess a mind. I am invisible, understand, simply because people refuse to see me."[39] The phrase "behold the invisible" suggests this sense of invisibility described by the narrator. With only glasses and a hat, he becomes the seen unseen and is rendered invisible.

During the Coagula process, again, true to the tenets of the torture porn film, Chris asks Jim, "Why us? Why Black people?" The art dealer shrugs dismissively and offers a reply that is perfectly in keeping with neoliberal race doctrines: "I don't know. Color doesn't matter to me. What I'm after is something … deeper. I want you eye, man." What is this deeper thing to which Chris' would-be master refers? Is it not an opportunity to gain access to the power of the white gaze? While it may seem contradictory to suggest that taking possession of Chris' body would open a channel for Jim to regain the white gaze and reenter its visual field of power, it is in fact precisely this contradiction that signals what is truly terrifying about the Coagula process and Chris' predicament. As Yancy contends, "the Black body is the sacrificial object, the fantasized projection that whiteness relies upon to remain, sutured, whole, intact."[40]

Jim is the perfect emblem of colorblindness in a neoliberal world. He literally does not see color, but is acutely aware of Chris' Blackness and the possibilities afforded by taking possession of it. Returning to Hartman,

If the black body is the vehicle of the other's power, pleasure, and profit, then it is no less true that it is the white or near-white body that makes the captive's suffering visible and discernible. Indeed, the elusiveness of Black suffering can be attributed to a racist optics in which black flesh is itself identified as the source of opacity, the denial of black humanity, and the effacement of sentience integral to the wanton use of the captive body.[41]

Here we see why Jim never had "the eye." He does not seem to register that these qualities are inseparable and that the ground of any artist's work begins in the body. Put simply, there is no Black "aesthetic" without Blackness. Black consciousness and the web of culture and history from which it is spawned and spun is embedded in the sinuous fibers of that body and cannot be torn one from the other.

One of the crucial problems raised in *Get Out* addresses how we understand linkages between racism and the Black body. If racism at the level of the body is the expression of revulsion at the appearance of the other grounded in forms of difference, how does the Coagula process, where master and slave are psychically split but made physically one, reconcile the ontological collapse of this difference? What *Get Out* makes clear is that Blackness does not suffer from surface invisibilities: Black skin, Black bodies, Black musculature; these things are not invisible, they are *hyper-visible*. In fact, they are so visible they exceed what they are in themselves. They signify all that traffics in the realm of the fantasmatic: desires, fears, wishes, and projections. Unlike the auction blocks of the eighteenth and nineteenth centuries where Black men, women and children were sold into slavery under colonial/capitalist pretenses on the basis of their capacity for physical labor to harvest crops, tend fields, and other forms of brute menial labor, the modern day auction block of *Get Out* is a screen on which the bidders project their desires, fantasies, and insecurities, alongside their physical failings, infirmities and incapacities. And true to the arc of American history, whiteness will remedy these weaknesses through a parasitic attachment to Blackness.

Runaway Slave

Chris is now, in no uncertain terms, a runaway slave. Chris begins his escape by cleverly picking cotton (yes, picking cotton) from the armchair he is bound to and stuffing it in his ears to prevent paralysis from the sound of the spoon scraping against the teacup coming from the television. He strikes Jeremy unconscious with a bocce ball, kills Dean with the horns of a buck's head still mounted to a plaque, kills Missy, and faces-off with Jeremy a second time, killing him and taking the keys to the white Porsche from the film's opening sequence used to abduct Andre. As Chris is fighting his way out of the sunken place, then out of the basement of "black mold," Rose sits on her bed sipping milk from a straw and nibbling on cereal while on her laptop perusing a database of Black athletes in the NCAA. The scene forms a rhyming couplet with our introduction to Rose looking over the pastries in the glass display case in the Stay Woke sequence. In worlds of white privilege all options are available, everything is for the taking, and all wants and desires are measurably within reach. Black people in the world of *Get Out* are, like pastries in a glass case, objects to be looked over, ruminated upon, and acquired. And to make certain nothing is left to subtly the photos Chris discovered of Rose with other Black captives in the closet now appear hung on the wall in the background above her bed. We can see now that Rose is a hunter, a gameswoman who, like all who track, stalk and kill for sport, enjoys being surrounded by mementos from her conquests. It is a clever bit of thematic irony that Chris should dismount a hunting trophy from the wall of the Armitage game room and use it to kill her father.

Chris attempts to escape in the white Porsche while calling 911 dispatch for help, but Georgina jumps in front of the car before he can get away. Chris hits her with the car triggering the guilt from his inaction on the night of his mother's death. Chris stops the car and here we see two generic characteristics of Black character typology come into conflict: his intuition and his trauma. In yet another example of "I know very well, but ... " (he literally says to himself. "No, no, don't fuckin' do it. Just go.") the burden of guilt proves too great, and Chris makes two questionable choices. First, he curiously decides to end his call with the 911 operator to whom he was explaining his emergency (if one can think of running away from a plantation in terms of emergency: "911, what's your emergency?" "I'm a runaway slave escaping the Armitage plantation, send the police to help me!"), and second, he exits the vehicle and retrieves Georgina who is unconscious from the collision and places her in the car beside him.

Rose, who is now aware of the situation and has presumably seen the corpses of her family, true to hunter form steps on to the porch with a bolt-action rifle to shoot Chris. Unable to lineup a shot, she stoically lowers the weapon and upon seeing Georgina in the car says, "Grandma." With the matrilineal link between Rose and Georgina/Grandma confirmed, we cut back to the cabin of the car. As Georgina/Grandma slowly regains consciousness, her wig slips off revealing the surgical scar from the coagula procedure. What happens next is unexpected and worth unpacking. Georgina/Grandma turns to Chris and, of all things, screams, "You ruined my house!" Before attacking Chris who accidentally collides with a tree, killing her on impact. It is a stunning declaration in light of the fact that Georgina/Grandma knows that her progeny are dead or dying and the entire Armitage operation has been laid to waste. The statement returns us again to Cheng's comparative reading of *Parasite* and *Get Out* and her question "Having your body stolen is surely more traumatic than having your house stolen ... or is it?" Clearly, for Grandma Armitage, home is where the heart is, and the destruction of her possessions and property would seem to be the most traumatic occurrence in a unicum of violence and ruination for her family. The destruction of the Armitage property is the destruction of everything it signifies: generational wealth, class status, property ownership, and a privileged, proprietary site for perpetuating the theft, sale, and enslavement of Black bodies. As it turns out, in worlds of white privilege a lost home is indeed the most traumatic loss of all.

Chris limps exhaustedly from the car dodging gunfire from Rose who has run from the porch to the road with her rifle. Unable to hit Chris, Walter/Grandpa runs out from behind Rose and chases Chris down. He tackles, straddles, and seizes Chris by the skull, but Chris quick-thinkingly deploys the camera flash from his phone to break the hypnotic spell cast upon him and allow the sunken Black consciousness to regain control of its body. What transpires in these final few minutes of the film is nothing less than devastating. The Black man, whose identity is unknown to us, turns to face Rose. He, like Chris, is her ex-lover in whom he once confided and trusted; with whom he once shared embraces and physical intimacy; who, like Chris, was bamboozled and broken to make way for whiteness. With stunning composure he tells Rose, "Let me do it," and reaches out for her rifle. Rose hands it to the man she thinks is her grandfather, but in reality she is handing the weapon to the Black man she helped to annihilate through emotional and physical rape, psychological manipulation, and eventually trans/plantation. The moment he takes hold of the gun, he shoots Rose in the abdomen. Rose falls stunned onto the road, her white blouse soaked in blood. The man turns to face Chris and without saying a word loads another round into the chamber of the rifle. With a single teardrop streaking down his cheek and without hesitation, he places the barrel of the rifle under his chin and kills himself.

In desperation, Rose makes one last attempt to retrieve the rifle, but Chris pulls it from her limp grasp and straddles her. This whole exchange is comprised of fifteen shots set in a shot-reverse shot pattern and in it seems crystallized in miniature the central dramas of Black and white in America. Rose immediately reverts back to the woman Chris thought he knew, the woman to whom only hours earlier by the lake he declared his love for, saying, "You're all I've got. I'm not going to leave here without you, I'm not going to abandon you." Bookending the embrace that began the weekend in the doorway of Chris' apartment, Rose whimpers to him, "Chris, I'm so sorry. It's me. And I love you." Chris nods wordlessly at

Rose and takes hold of her neck and squeezes. While strangling her, Rose's expression changes from a grimace to a spiteful smile. Seeing the smile, Chris releases the hold on her neck and freed from his death grip her smile falls away. What follows happens for only a few brief seconds, but it is, simply put, one of the most powerful moments in any American film and one of the very few instances in the history of Hollywood cinema where a Black person and a white person exchange a bare, authentic, intersubjective look.

Chris looks down at Rose crestfallen; his expression twisted from pain, dejection, and melancholy. Given the pace of narrative events and all that he has been subjected to during his escape, from being stabbed in the hand with a letter opener by Missy to being strangled by Jeremy, then surviving a head on car collision with a tree and being tackled and attacked by Walter/Grandpa, it is the first moment Chris has had a chance to take account of the part of his body that hurts the most—his broken heart. Rose looks back at Chris as if looking at something or someone she has never seen before and is not equipped to recognize. Rose is left face-to-face in an inescapable encounter with the rawness of Chris' pain. In this moment, it could be the first time in her life she has *seen* a Black person. On the cusp of death, facing Chris, she is made to *behold the invisible*.

But Rose has one more card to play. The spell of their exchange is dissipated by the arrival of a patrol car. With only its siren lights flashing, Rose and Chris have diametrically opposed responses that align perfectly with life in Black America Now. Rose turns and says, "Help. Help me,"[42] while Chris, on the other hand, simply pushes up to his knees and raises his hands in the air. It is shattering to see Chris, an innocent Black man, kneeling with his hands up (like all young Black people learn when given "the talk") in hopes of not being shot and killed by police, and to see Rose reach into her "invisible knapsack" and exploit her white privilege to cry for help. The implication of what is likely to come is clear: Rose will be deemed the victim in the situation because it is what her whiteness affords her, and Chris will be held guilty on multiple counts of murder without the least consideration that he is in fact the victim and is fighting for his survival.

We are reminded here of the incident described in the previous chapter when Amy Cooper played the *other* race card and threatened the innocent Black man in front of her by telling him, "I'm going to call the cops and tell them an African American is threatening my life." This is the same card Rose tries to play when she sees the sirens and calls for help. Knowing very well it is the trump card in America's racial deck, Chris does not bother attempting to state his case and begins executing the protocols of "the talk" (keep your hands where the police can see them, don't make any sudden movements, etc.). One of the key lessons of Afropessimism is that the violence saturating Black life cannot be eliminated through exposure. The fact that Cooper knew she was being openly recorded on video and remained undeterred in uttering lies of being threatened by the very Black man recording her illustrates how exposing the structural conditions of violence in Black life offers no assurance of prevention. As a Black man living in America, Chris knows that in any encounter with institutional authority, regardless of circumstances, the die has already been cast.

The twist, of course, is that the car is not a police car, but an airport security car, and it is not the police but Rod who has arrived to rescue Chris. Barely able to muster an expression of relief, Chris rises to his feet without saying a word and gets into Rod's car. Peele's use of Rod's arrival in a TSA car is a masterstroke of audience manipulation and strategic levity, for almost in the same moment in which we are presented with the worst possible outcome we are given the best possible outcome. (But, really, we are only left with the worst possible outcome.) Rod proffers the predictable humor we expect from his character, but Chris, aside from asking how he found him, remains silent, looking blankly out of the passenger side window. The movie ends.

The realization Chris must face, what is contained in the final shot of him driving away from the Armitage estate, his eyes vacant and searching, is that there was never a turning point for him, never a fork in the road, never a set of choices to be made; there is no backstory against which the events in the narrative or the violence Chris experiences can be set into a logical matrix of means and ends or cause and effect. In the language of Afropessimism, Chris' predicament is ontological; which is to say before Chris was born to the mother who would die in the rain on the street outside her home neglected by a driver who did not think her body or her life meaningful enough to stop the car that struck her down, his fate had been decided: he was, as Imbram X. Kendi might put it, "stamped from the beginning."[43] What the final brother comes to discover is that there was no "normality" to begin with and thus there is no "normality" to restore; there is no possibility of a return to equilibrium. While the horror genre's "final girl" invariably faces the reality that the monster is unkillable and that which is repressed must return, a prelapsarian world exists in which restoration is at least conceivable. Her birthright is "normality" and it is this "normality" she fights for, a fight her survival signifies. What makes the final brother's fight for survival aporetic is that the survival he fights for is essentially hollow for there is no world that he might return to or restore. The forces that oppress him are woven into the tapestry of his world and cannot come undone without the world as he knows it disintegrating. Again, we return here to Wilderson who points out that, "The narrative arc of the slave who is Black (unlike the generic slave who may be of any race) is not a narrative arc at all, but a flat line of 'historical stillness': a flat line that 'moves' from disequilibrium to a moment in the narrative of faux-equilibrium, to disequilibrium restored and/or rearticulated."[44]

Here Walter's suicide comes into sharper focus. In a dark twist on DuBoisian "double consciousness," the Coagula process suspends Black being in the liminal state between seeing with one's own eyes and seeing through the eyes of the other. As a "passenger" in his own body displaced by a colonizing white consciousness he was made a passive witness to the institutionalized practice of New World slavery, but what is also made apparent is the extent to which whiteness and Blackness are not markers of corporeally determined states, but structural positions and systemic paradigms that can achieve wholesale reversals with the smallest of conscious pivots (To say: This Black person in front of me is not Black, it is really a white person). The frightening implication is that he is allowed to see through the looking glass (a trope of the sc-fi/horror hybrid like the sunglasses in John Carpenter's *They Live* (1988), or more pointedly the procedure Black people undergo in the German film *Transfer* (2010), a predecessor to *Get Out*, in which elderly, wealthy white people buy Black bodies to inhabit them and prolong their lives) to see what it is to be looked upon by white gazes that see him (vertiginously) not as Black, but as white ("to see oneself being seen"). This is what it means to be Black and to stare into an abyss that stares back.

Walter knows there is nothing to be done, nothing to be restored, and so, without a second thought, as if bringing to fruition Kilmonger's words to T'Challa, he knows death is better than bondage. And this point is a crucial one to make because Peele had originally intended to end the film with a Black man left in bondage.

Afterlife ...

In the film's alternate ending (what was, in fact, its original ending), Chris straddles Rose and as he begins strangling her she breaks into that spiteful smile, but instead of releasing his grip, Chris strangles her to death. In the moment her smile dissolves and she takes her last breath, the police (not Rod) arrive and arrest Chris. The following scene is one we see frequently in American films populated with Black characters: Rod is visiting Chris in prison and they speak to each other on a correctional telephone through a glass partition. Rod tries to impress upon Chris the importance of remembering what happened that weekend at the Armitage house, but a dejected

Chris simply says, "I'm good. I stopped it." He puts the phone down, walks away, and is taken back to his cell where he will remain indefinitely. The film foregrounds in an all too familiar way the sense that for Black people the passage from childhood to adulthood is a journey in which the formation of Black subjectivity/Black identity develops squarely within the coordinates of trauma.

How is it that so many Black bodies have been disappeared? What can we learn about the vulnerability of Black life in the present from the manner and method Black bodies are captured and cast into New World slavery to a colonizing white consciousness? What happens when we are made acutely aware that systems of power and wealth in America anticipate Black death and have in place mechanisms to profit from the subjugation and fungibility of Black bodies? How can Black life be lived in the face of this material fact and the impact of its full realization? One of the questions the film poses is how will Chris be left to live his life in the aftermath of his attempted abduction? How does this young, Black man now navigate a world he knows sees him as a fungible commodity; his body something upon which claims can be made and possession seized? What does Chris do with the knowledge that, as Sharpe concludes, "This is black life in the wake; this is the flesh, these are the bodies, to which anything and everything can be done."[45] Finally, where does the final brother go?

The tagline for Tobe Hooper's *The Texas Chainsaw Massacre* is "Who will survive and what will be left of them?" This line, in its simplicity, has remained the genre's definitive question, but in race horror films the possible responses available and the conditions of survivability appear to be in direct opposition. *Get Out*'s alternate ending offers a glimpse into another possibility (the one all too common in everyday Black life) for Chris and his life after the attempted abduction by the Armitage family and his brush with New World slavery. However, the ending Peele devised in its place is everywhere more sophisticated, more complex, and more nuanced. Not for the obvious reasons of mood and tone in telling the story (it puts a heavy pall of somberness over the movie, which is saying quite a bit), or for the fact that to see Chris remain pliant and unassertive as he was in all of his encounters with white people during the weekend at the Armitage estate ("I'm good" is another version of "It's fine"), but it raises a more difficult question: how will Chris continue to live in Black America Now? This, in a sense, is the more difficult ending. What we are left with is a broken Black man who is forever changed in an America that remains unchanged. In the ending for the film's theatrical release, without having to see Chris surrender to a lifetime of wrongful imprisonment, there is no mistaking that Black trauma will endure, that systems of white supremacy remain, and the auction attendees have returned to their manicured suburban neighborhoods like the one from the film's opening sequence where Andre is abducted. They will wake up to a new day that is just the same for them as it was before.

We are familiar with the story of the arrest and imprisonment of Black men and how Black bodies get caught up in the gears of the prison industrial complex. The more difficult story to tell is Black trauma in perpetuity. This is why *Get Out* is for me the first masterpiece of "wake work" in this early century of American cinema: Chris is living in the wake of his mother's death, in the wake of transatlantic slavery, in the wake of Jim Crow, in the wake of Obama's presidency and the fata morgana of post-racial unity it conjured, and in the wake of countless acts of state sanctioned police brutality and murder against Black people that have reinvigorated Black social justice movements across the country. By the film's end, he will now have to live in the wake of another shattering trauma and to process not only the delinking of an attachment to another loved one in death, but his fundamental delinking from the world as he knows it.

In the last analysis, though the film begins with the Childish Gambino song "*Redbone*" and its pleas to "stay woke," it could very well have ended with the repeated declarations that resonate throughout a different Childish Gambino track: "*This is America*."

CONCLUSION

I began this book by proposing mutually illuminative links between contemporary critical race theory and Jordan Peele's *Get Out*. I have underscored key terms that have gained traction in recent years among critical race theorists whose work examines the veiled logics of transatlantic slavery in the present and the permutations of anti-Black racism it gives rise to. My goal has been to select terms that best describe the plight facing Chris Washington as he fights for his survival and is left to face the existential magnitude of its aftermath. The combination of critical race theory and close analysis of *Get Out* together has generated a harrowing snapshot of Black America Now. I have described how the film's release coincided with growing outrage in the Black community physically and spiritually fatigued by brazen acts of police brutality against Black people that ultimately gave rise to the Black Lives Matter movement. Through the end of the Obama administration and across the four years of the Trump presidency, the structural disenfranchisement of Black people has remained a focal point in all areas of American life. In making *Get Out* conversant with contemporary critical race theory we can see how the film's success and its cultural impact intersect with the many social challenges Black people face in the historical present.

There is little disputing the profound influence *Get Out* has had on the American horror film. In fact, it has singlehandedly ignited a renaissance in Black horror filmmaking. Since the release of *Get Out* there have been numerous Black cast horror films and television shows that focus on the Black experience (*Us* [2019], *Bad Hair* [2020], *Candyman* [2021], *Antebellum* [2020], *The Twilight Zone* [2019], *Lovecraft Country* [2020], and *Horror Noire* (2021) to name a few). It is not surprising that at the center of this new wave of horror production the themes of slavery, police brutality, and social death persist. To repeat Due's remark on Black issues in the context of the horror film, "Black history is black horror."

There is nothing sentimental about *Get Out*. It does not pretend to imagine a scenario in which the shattered world of its protagonist might be recomposed into its illusory formation prior to rupture. Consistent with the film's nihilistic denouement, it would be disingenuous to conclude the discussion elaborated in this book with a gesture toward uplift or to attempt to light a path out from the darkness at the heart of the film by insisting critical race theory offers affordances for such a change in itinerary. *Get Out* is very clearly a film determined to chart white supremacy's unmaking of a Black world unknowingly adrift in orbit of other shattered Black worlds. To do this it whitewashes the auction block and the operations of plantation slavery and reimagines it for a neoliberal present. With that said, it has not been my intention to portray critical race theory as a discourse that is unilaterally nihilistic. But in allowing the story of *Get Out* to decide appropriate terminology for close analysis, critical race theory clearly makes available a powerful set of descriptive tools compatible with the film's somber depiction of Black life under neoliberal white supremacy. It needs pointing out, though (even if only briefly), that critical race theory as a humanist discipline and framework for interrogating the relations between Black life and the modern world is not singularly focused on the social death of Blackness.

In contrast to narratives of Black death and a concerted focus on the afterlives of slavery, much important work is being done in critical race theory that foregrounds the vitality of Black life despite existential conditions meant to foreshorten its flourishing. For example, in the recently published book *Black Aliveness, or a Poetics of Being*, Kevin Quashie sets out to "imagine a black world" in order to make space "for one to engage black being-in-the-world beyond the imperatives of anti-Blackness and the restrictions of ideas about blackness."[1]

He cautions while anti-Blackness is an inseparable dimension of Blackness under the structural oppression of white supremacy, to focus on subjection as definitive of Black life is to confirm Black being through negation.

Alternatively, Quashie proposes the concept of "aliveness" as a method for conceiving Blackness as something outside the coordinates of anti-Blackness. In Quashie's view, "It is undeniable that every historical thing, including the days of summer 2020, reminds us that Blackness, terror, and death are synonyms in the world. That sentence needs to stand alone, and so does this next one: in the world of a black person's being, death is both a fact of antiblack threat and a fact of being alive."[2] Quashie expresses this sense of aliveness as a "world" and insists upon the power of Black world making as an ameliorative strategy against having to insistently qualify Black existence through negation. He writes, "In a black world, black people are human without qualification. In a black world orientation, there is no need to verify Blackness along any measure, especially since such a world is not instantiated in response to a problem. A black world *is* …."[3]

It is erroneous to assume that the field of critical race theory and the political and artistic practices to which it runs adjacent are focused solely on the linkages between death and Blackness. Stressing this point is especially crucial in the present moment as signs of weariness in both progressive and conservative camps arising from, presumably, too much attention being dedicated to Black life and Black issues begins to set in. Recent expressions of this weariness have, rather remarkably, come in the form of attacking critical race theory by name.

"Unsanctioned Narratives"

Earlier in Chapter 1, I described conservative attacks on teaching critical race theory in school classrooms. I want to look more closely at one example. On March 18, 2021, in a news conference outlining a new statewide civics curriculum, Florida Governor

Ron Desantis, to smattering applause, insisted that the program "will expressly exclude unsanctioned narratives like critical race theory and other unsubstantiated theories." Governor Desantis would go on to explain, "There is no room in our classrooms for things like critical race theory teaching kids to hate their country and to hate each other is not worth one red cent of taxpayer money."[4] Unbothered by the absence of evidence or explanation to support his claims (not that reason, logic, or merit matter in political theater), Desantis calls upon critical race theory to serve as the straw man to advance an anti-Black agenda and signal political opposition to gaining momentum nationwide for racial justice, social equity, and the recognition of Black life as human life. In a turn of cartoonish irony, labeling critical race theory—a discursive practice primarily written by Black people about Black experience—as an "unsanctioned narrative" is, quite literally, the sort of anti-Black discrimination the field of critical race theory means to redress.

Some questions come immediately to mind. How, exactly, was the determination made that critical race theory is or should be unsanctioned? Or, better still, if critical race theory were to make its appeal to be a "sanctioned narrative," to which governing body would it plead its case? What would be the radius of this governing body's jurisdiction? In other words, where would the threshold between sanctioned and unsanctioned lie? How does the power to delegitimize an entire intellectual discipline and its rich history with ties to legal and political discourse, and intellectual and artistic production come about? If a large portion of the work produced in contemporary critical race theory utilizes the memoir format in order to draw directly from the personal histories of Black authors who seek to ground their critical interventions in material life, does declaring these stories "unsanctioned narratives" not also elide these personal histories? But, then again, is it not the case that the true purpose of these curricular modifications is to bring about these wreckages?

Also implied in the curtailing of race pedagogy is the disenfranchisement of teachers and scholars of color who are professionally trained and personally invested in the issues critical race theory addresses. By designating an entire field of study "unsanctioned" and declaring wholesale that the vast literature comprising the field are "unsubstantiated theories," Desantis' edict seeks to delegitimize those trained in this area of thought who have contributed to the field through personal testimony and rigorous research, and who remain invested in advancing the issues central to its doctrines.

In this nebulous injunction against critical race theory and the purported risks it poses to "make kids hate each other and hate their country," which texts would be open to censure? Clearly a book such as this with "critical race theory" in its title poses a clear and present danger to school children everywhere and should immediately be flung upon the nearest pyre, but would the poetry of Audre Lorde or the fiction of Toni Morrison also be deemed "unsanctioned" because of the way these authors address race or call attention to histories of oppression and the structural disenfranchisement of Black life in worlds of white privilege? What about Jordan Peele's *Get Out*? Surely its ideas, too, are unsanctioned and its content unsubstantiated.[5] What is at stake here is how we orient ourselves to questions of racism and its effects and the more insidious forms it takes when political power on the one hand denies its racism through rhetorical misdirection, while simultaneously instituting programs that work to ingrain marginalization and enforce laws that overtly promote and propagate racism. Or, more insidiously, disavows its existence by whitewashing school curriculum and curtailing speech acts that aim to call attention to the brutal legacies of slavery, Jim Crow, and other forms of systemic racism that everywhere continue to pervade Black America Now.

In an essay titled "The Humanities in the Age of Loneliness," Robert D. Newman insists we need to overcome "a culture and politics of blame and grievance to form a revolutionary idealism based on the collective. Any passionate renewal of our commitment to the general welfare requires that we focus on the ideals and identity we share rather than venting grievances that divide us."[6] How do we negotiate this call to suspend the pursuit of grievances from oppressed populations as a measure toward a reconciliatory politics that does not hinge on the suppression of Black articulations of pain and suffering like those found in Desantis' attempt to eliminate critical race theory from Florida State curriculum? Does healing require a period in which grief and its expressions are allowable or even necessary? If so, what is clear is that only now do we seem to be collectively entering that period of grieving by openly insisting that Black life matters.

Expressing grief in the presence of those who have wrought harm (directly or indirectly) upon the grieving requires that the harm-doers recognize and acknowledge unconditionally the legitimacy of the griever's grief. This typically requires harm-doers (or the structurally advantaged who profit in the present from pain wrought upon others in the past) to enter into a space of discomfort for and with the structurally disadvantaged. The harm-doer must do so willingly and extend to the harmed the time needed to grieve. The path along any road of reconciliation is paved by such gestures. It is unimaginable to me how we collectively move forward otherwise.

Welcome to the Desert of the Real

The stark revelations that come into view for Chris after he leaves the Armitage estate and is irrevocably delinked from his former world is analogous to an iconic moment from the Wachowski sister's *The Matrix* (1999). At the end of the film's first act, Thomas Anderson (a.k.a. Neo)—who by day is a low-level office worker and by night a cyberpunk hacker—is introduced to Morpheus (Laurence Fishburne), a man he is told can answer the question that plagues him most: *what is the matrix?* In this encounter, Morpheus and Neo share an exchange in which Morpheus explains:

> MORPHEUS: It is the world that has been pulled over your eyes to blind you from the truth.

NEO: What truth?

MORPHEUS: That you are a slave, Neo. You were born into bondage, born into a prison that you cannot smell, or taste, or touch; a prison for your mind.

Morpheus tells Neo that the "matrix" can only be grasped if seen with one's own eyes. He offers Neo a blue pill and a red pill: taking the blue pill will erase the memory of their meeting and Neo will go back to his life as it was before; on the other hand (literally), taking the red pill marks the first step toward discovering what the "matrix" is and what it means. Neo, of course, takes the red pill and wakes up in a post-apocalyptic world annihilated by global warfare between humans and machines.

After Neo has sufficiently recovered from his "awakening," Morpheus takes Neo into a computer program called "The Construct" where he explains the world that he has known is nothing more than a simulation created by Artificial Intelligence to distract humans whose bodies from birth are kept in liquid-filled incubators and used as an energy source for the machines until the body's life force expires. Seated in front of a tube television set—one eerily similar to the television set in the basement of the Armitage home where Chris, like Neo, is exposed to the reality of his bondage—Morpheus shows Neo familiar images: a cityscape, a crowded sidewalk, traffic moving along a freeway. He explains that the world he lived in was nothing more than a neural interactive simulation called "the matrix." "You've been living in a dream world, Neo," says Morpheus before changing the channel on the television one final time with the preface: "This is the world as it exists today." On the television screen the image of a completely scorched cityscape flickers into view as the camera closes in, absorbing Morpheus and Neo into the image. Finally, Morpheus turns to Neo and declares, "Welcome to the desert of the real." So, *what is the matrix?* Consonant with American war doctrines, it is a world secretly dependent upon Black people (Morpheus, a Black man; The Oracle, a Black woman, and the other minorities comprising the resistance and protecting the last bastion of freedom named Zion, no less) called upon to fight to restore a world from which they are fundamentally excluded, and if ever restored again to what it was before would no doubt continue to extend this exclusion indefinitely.

In the age of the machines, Neo is born into slavery and his body is used as a fungible energy source so that his oppressors can sustain their dominance and power-over-life. The truth of Neo's condition is elaborately hidden from him in a large-scale simulacrum duping him into believing he is free and his life is his own to author. The discovery that the world he has been living in is a material fiction shatters his perception of reality (which is also to say, shatters his ontology) and he must relearn in every way what it means to be human if he is to survive in "the desert of the real."

The similarities between *The Matrix* and *Get Out* (and their protagonists) are raised here not so much because either elucidates the other as because seen together they help clarify the clandestine workings of neo-slavery in the present. Recall that one of the core tenets of Afropessimism maintains that the rejuvenation and renewal of whiteness is dependent upon the destruction of Blackness, and that "Blackness is coterminous with slaveness."[7] If Blackness is coterminous with slaveness, Chris is *ipso facto* born into bondage, and if recalibrated forms of slaveness are to operate in a neoliberal post-racial society, the ontological terror of Black bondage must be disguised. To this end, the action of *Get Out*'s plot might be summarized as follows: By elaborating a social fiction of freedom, racial integration, and equal access to life, liberty, and the pursuit of happiness, white supremacy masquerades in colorblind drag and hides in plain sight until the rejuvenation and renewal of whiteness requires, even if only briefly, that its true form be exposed to its victims.

Despite their similarities, there is a crucial difference in the existential predicaments of Chris and Neo that underscores a key point reiterated throughout this book. Neo fights to restore a world that holds forth the possibility of a return to a time prior to rupture. So while he enters the desert of the real and his psychic integrity is broken by the impact of the truth of his condition, he (quite literally, as The One) embodies the possibility of a restoration of life before the rupture. True to the formula of the final brother, for Chris, his entering the desert of the real is precisely what Dionne Brand describes as passing through the door of no return. In a second alternate ending one imagines it is Morpheus and not Rod who arrives to take Chris away from the Armitage estate, and rather than Rod's attempt to layer humor over devastation with the line "Consider this situation, fuckin' handled," it is Morpheus who turns to Chris invitingly and says, "Welcome to the desert of the real." Chris sitting in the passenger side of Rod's TSA vehicle, his body exhausted and rigid, his eyes darting around at the world outside, has entered a desert of the real I have been calling Black America Now: a world pulled over his eyes leading him to believe he is a free and sentient Black man, but is revealed to be a mirage blinding him from the truth. That truth—to paraphrase Morpheus—is that he has been living in a dream (maybe even Martin Luther King Jr.'s "Dream") in which the possibility of inclusion, equity, and social integration seemed within reach when, in reality, in Black America Now, Chris was, is, and will always be looked upon as a slave in a world that is, ideologically, as scorched and blasted as the one Morpheus unveils to Neo.

The story of *Get Out* is a story of traumatic awakening. It does not deal with the historical legacies of slavery as such. *Get Out* tells the story of coming into the knowledge that Black subjectivity and Black life are socially (which is to say, structurally) invalidated—the social death of Blackness. It tells the story of a moment of reckoning. It does not offer us a past to reflect upon or a future to imagine, it places us instead in a traumatic present in which Black worlds are everywhere unmade. On this account, *Get Out* is truly a film of its time. Over the past decade we have seen Black worlds blown apart on our television screens, mobile screens, and in our social media feeds. At every moment when I thought this book complete, a Black person was murdered by police or killed by proxies armed with weapons and white privilege, an act of overt racism would roil public perception of what it means to live Black life in America, or fresh protests would erupt in cities across the country, intensifying on-going demands for racial justice (as I write this sentence, Derek Chauvin has been convicted of the murder of George Floyd and protests have erupted in response to the murder of another Black man: 20-year-old Daunte Wright).

What became starkly apparent is that this project could have been delayed indefinitely if every new state sanctioned Black murder or high-profile episode of racism or anti-Blackness captured on video were to be included in my attempt to fasten the work of contemporary critical race theory to the historical present as it is reflected in Jordan Peele's *Get Out*. It is precisely this theme of Black subjugation in perpetuity that is central to the work of critical race theorists; it is also the kernel at the heart of Peele's film. Once I was able to embrace this somewhat nihilistic proposition, this work found its end point, which is to say that it recognized that there is no end point in sight.

I am left with the feeling that I wish the events, both real and fictional, described in these pages never occurred and did not require consideration. Put differently, I wish this book never needed to be written. It seems to me that the end game of critical race theory—that is, its chief objective—is achieving its own elimination, meaning that even in its most nihilistic sense it yearns for a world in which it doesn't exist. To that end, this book is not a fire, but kindling for a fire that needs extinguishing.

NOTES

Introduction

1 See Andrew Monument's documentary *Nightmares in Red, White and Blue: The Evolution of the American Horror Film* (2009).

2 Aaron Kerner, *Torture Porn in the Wake of 9/11: Horror, Exploitation, and the Cinema of Sensation* (New Jersey: Rutgers University Press, 2015).

3 Following Touré's decision to capitalize the word "Black" in the Author's Note to his book, *Who's Afraid of Post-Blackness? What It Means to Be Black Now*, I, too, capitalize the word "Black" throughout this book as a way of emphasizing not only "a sense of ethnic cohesion," but something approaching a kind of experiential cohesion as well.

4 See Tananarive Due's foreword to Jordan Peele's published script for *Get Out* (Inventory Press) titled, "Get Out and the Black Horror Aesthetic," 7.

5 See Erica R. Edwards, Roderick A. Ferguson, and Jeffrey O. G. Ogbar (eds), *Keywords for African American Studies* (New York: New York University Press, 2018).

Chapter 1

1 "What Is Critical Race Theory?" *The New York Times*, July 9, 2021; "What Critical Race Theory Is ... and Isn't," CNN May 10, 2021; "What Is Critical Race Theory and Why Is It under Attack?" *Education Week*, May 18, 2021; and, "What is critical race theory and why do Republicans want to ban it from schools?" *The Washington Post*, May 29, 2021; "What Is Critical Race Theory?" *Fox News*, May 14, 2021.

2   https://www.youtube.com/watch?v=vxTMNu31DHU&t=113s.

3   "The Critical Race Theory Panic Has White People Afraid
    That They Might Be Complicit in Racism," CNN, July 8,
    2021: https://www.cnn.com/2021/07/06/us/critical-race-theory-
    philadelphia/index.html.

4   Eric Hobsbawm, *The Age of Extremes: A History of the World,
    1914–1991* (New York: Vintage Books, 1996), 3.

5   Carol Anderson, *White Rage: The Unspoken Truth of Our
    Racial Divide* (New York: Bloomsbury USA, 2016), 4.

6   See W.E.B. DuBois, *The Souls of Black Folk* (Chicago: A.C. McClurg
    & Co, 1903). DuBois uses the term "color line" in reference to
    proliferating forms of racial segregation and discrimination in the
    United States after the ostensible abolition of slavery.

7   https://www.youtube.com/watch?v=LZYsW_PxWAM. Accessed
    on July 30, 2021.

8   Deborah Douglas, "Obama's 'beer summit' Derailed Him on
    Race: Column," *USA Today*, July 20, 2016.

9   Jamelle Bouie, "After the 'beer summit,' the Fallacy of a
    Postracial America Was Over—and White Citizens Never
    Thought of Barack Obama the Same Way Again." Slate.com,
    September 21, 2016.

10 https://www.pewsocialtrends.org/2016/06/27/2-views-of-race-
    relations/.

11 "The Injustice of This Moment Is Not an 'Aberration'," *The
    New York Times*, Sunday Review, January 17, 2020.

12 https://blacklivesmatter.com/herstory/.

13 Keeanga-Yamahtta Taylor, *From #Blacklivesmatter to Black
    Liberation* (Chicago: Haymaker Books, 2016), 25.

14 Alessandra Raengo, *Critical Race Theory and Bamboozled*
    (Bloomsbury, 2016), 3.

15 Orlando Patterson, *Slavery and Social Death: A Comparative
    Study* (Cambridge: Harvard University Press, 1982), preface ix.

16 Saidiya Hartman, *Scenes of Subjection: Terror, Slavery, and
    Self-Making in Nineteenth Century America* (New York:
    Oxford University Press, 1997), 65. Hartman observes: "The
    slave is neither civic man nor free worker but excluded from
    the narrative of 'we the people' that effects the linkage of the
    modern individual to the state … ."

17 Calvin Warren, *Ontological Terror: Blackness, Nihilism,
    Emancipation* (Durham: Duke University Press, 2018), 12.

18 Franz Fanon, *Black Skin, White Mask* (New York: Grove, 1952), 110.
19 Warren, 9.
20 Warren, 9.
21 Frank B. Wilderson III, *Afropessimism* (New York: Liveright Publishing Corporation, 2020), 228.
22 Wilderson, 102.
23 Jared Sexton, "Afropessimism: The Unclear Word", *Rhizomes: Cultural Studies in Emerging Knowledge*, (Issue 29, 2016). http://www.rhizomes.net/issue29/sexton.html
24 Wilderson, 15.
25 Wilderson, 17.
26 See Frank B. Wilderson III, *Red, White, and Black: Cinema and the Structure of U.S.Antagonisms* (Durham: Duke University Press, 2010).
27 Wilderson, *Afropessimism*, 41.
28 Jesse McCarthy, "On Afropessimism," *Los Angeles Review of Books*, July 20, 2019: https://lareviewofbooks.org/article/on-afropessimism/.
29 McCarthy, "On Afropessimism."
30 Wilderson, *Afropessimism*, 225.
31 Taylor, 49.
32 Wilderson, *Afropessimism*, 40.
33 https://www.oed.com/view/Entry/64098026
34 Ijeoma Oluo, *So You Want to Talk about Race* (New York: Seal Press, 2018), 169.
35 https://www.youtube.com/watch?v=9ufpU3X-t4w. Accessed on August 10, 2021.
36 Derald Wing Sue, *Microaggressions in Everyday Life: Race, Gender, and Sexual Orientations* (New Jersey: John Wiley & Sons, 2010), 164.
37 George Yancy, *Look, A White!: Philosophical Essays on Whiteness* (Philadelphia: Temple University Press, 2012), 31.
38 Yancy, 34.
39 Yancy, 34.
40 Yancy, 33.
41 Oluo, 169.
42 Lauren Berlant in an interview with Brad Evans titled, "Without Exception: On the Ordinariness of Violence," *Los Angeles*

Review of Books: https://lareviewofbooks.org/article/without-exception-on-the-ordinariness-of-violence/.

43 D.W. Sue, C.M. Capodilupo, and A.M.B. Holder, "Racial Microaggressions in the Life Experience of Black Americans," *Professional Psychology: Research and Practice* 39, no. 3 (2008): 335.

44 Richard Delgado and Jean Stefancic, *Critical Race Theory: An Introduction* (New York: New York University Press, 2012), 88.

45 Robin Diangelo, *White Fragility: Why It's So Hard For White People to Talk About Racism* (Boston: Beacon Press, 2018), 4.

46 Oluo, 63.

47 In *Black Bodies, White Gazes: The Continuing Significance of Race in America*, Yancy warns that if you are Black, "you can't afford to believe you are seen as a 'neoliberal subject' free from the force of white racism and its ugly legacy. You must not assume your life matters in the same way white lives matter. You must not assume that you are granted unconditional spatial mobility, you must not assume that you can exercise your right to defend your dignity through 'free speech' without dire consequences … The history of white supremacy in this country more than justifies my cautionary advice to you." George Yancy, *Black Bodies, White Gazes: The Continuing Significance of Race in America* (Lanham, Maryland: Rowman & Littlefield, 2017), xxii.

48 Roopali Mukherjee (eds. Erica R. Edwards, Roderick A. Ferguson, O. Jeffrey, and G. Ogbar) *Keywords For African American Studies* (New York: New York University Press), 161.

49 https://www.nytimes.com/2020/02/06/movies/oscarssowhite-history.html.

50 Taylor, 72.

51 These remarks were delivered by Gloria Ladson-Billings in a talk titled "Critical Race Theory and Education". The talk was given in April of 2015 at UNC Asheville. The full talk is available on YouTube: https://www.youtube.com/watch?v=katwPTn-nhE&t=1911s.

52 Todd McGowan, *Capitalism and Desire: The Psychic Cost of Free Markets* (New York: Columbia University Press, 2016), 79.

53 https://lucian.uchicago.edu/blogs/mediatheory/keywords/gaze/

54 bell hooks, *Black Looks: Race and Representation* (New York: Routledge, 2015), 116.

55 hooks, 115.

56   David Marriott, *On Black Men* (New York: Columbia University Press, 2000), 34.

57   Fanon, 92.

58   Fanon, 95.

59   Fanon, 92.

60   Marriott, ix.

61   Fanon, 95.

62   Yancy, xx.

63   Yancy, xxii.

64   Jayna Brown, (eds. Erica R. Edwards, Roderick A. Ferguson, and Jeffrey O. G. Ogbar), "Body," *Keywords for African American Studies* (New York: New York University Press), 29.

65   Yancy, xxx.

66   See Dorothy Roberts, *Killing the Black Body: Race, Reproduction, and the Meaning of Liberty* (New York: Vintage Books, 1999).

67   Patterson, 5.

68   Patterson, ix.

69   Hartman, 26.

70   William Melvin Kelley, "If You're Woke, You Dig It," *The New York Times*, May 20, 1962: https://timesmachine.nytimes.com/timesmachine/1962/05/20/140720532.pdf.

71   Kelley, "If You're Woke, You Dig It."

72   https://www.okayplayer.com/originals/georgia-muldrow-erykah-badu-stay-woke-master-teacher.html.

73   Damon Young, "In Defense of Wokeness," *New York Times*. November 29, 2019. https://www.nytimes.com/2019/11/29/opinion/woke-impeachment-trump.html

74   Young, "In Defense of Wokeness."

75   Saidiya Hartman, *Lose Your Mother: A Journey along the Atlantic Slave Route* (New York: Farrar, Straus and Giroux, 2007), 6. (emphasis mine).

76   Christina Sharpe, *In the Wake: On Blackness and Being* (Durham: Duke University Press, 2016), 15.

77   Sharpe, 7.

78   Sharpe, 14.

79   Sharpe, 14.

80   Sharpe, 18.

81   Sharpe, 14.

82 Sidney W. Mintz, "Caribbean Society," *International Encyclopedia of the Social Sciences*, ed. David L. Sills. Vol 2. (New York: Macmillan, 1968), 306–19. Web. May 1, 2017.

83 Sharpe, 30.

84 Kathryn Yusoff links this phenomenon to soil-based, geological processes. See *A Billion Black Anthropocenes or None* (Minneapolis: University of Minnesota Press, 2018), 38.

85 Achille Mbembe, *Necropolitics* (Durham: Duke University Press, 2019), 76.

86 Sharpe, 32.

87 Sharpe, 32.

88 Mbembe, 75.

89 Hartman, *Scenes of Subjection*, 21.

90 See Aviva Briefel and Sianne Ngai's excellent essay, "'How Much Did You Pay for This Place?' Fear, Entitlement, and Urban Space in Bernard Rose's *Candyman*".

91 Eric Lott, *Black Mirror: The Cultural Contradictions of American Racism* (Cambridge, MA: The Belknap Press of Harvard University Press, 2017), 26.

92 For this reason, it comes as little surprise that director Jordan Peele has written and produced a remake of *Candyman* (2021).

93 Robin Wood, *Hollywood From Vietnam to Reagan … and Beyond* (New York: Columbia University Press, 2003), 71.

94 Wilderson, *Afropessimism*, 226.

95 Wilderson, *Afropessimism*, 226.

Chapter 2

1 Wilderson, *Afropessimism*, 225.

2 "Get Out's Jordan Peele Responds to Golden Globes Category," *Deadline*, November 17, 2017: https://deadline.com/2017/11/jordan-peele-get-out-golden-globes-comedy-explanation-statement-1202211276/.

3 https://www.vulture.com/article/get-out-oral-history-jordan-peele.html.

4 Dawn Keetley, *Jordan Peele's Get Out: Political Horror* (Columbus: The Ohio State University Press, 2020), 3.

5 Robin Wood, "Introduction to the American Horror Film," in *Robin Wood On the Horror Film: Collected Essays and*

Reviews, ed. Barry Keith Grant (Detroit: Wayne State University Press, 2018), 77.

6   Wood, 78.

7   Marc Jancovich, *American Horror From 1951 to the Present* (Keele, Staffordshire: Keele University Press, 1994), 16.

8   Paul Wells, *The Horror Genre: From Beelzebub to Blair Witch* (London: Wallflower, 2000), 75.

9   Jancovich, 39.

10   Tananarive Due, "Get Out and the Black Horror Aesthetic" (Foreword), in Jordan Peele's *Get Out: The Complete Annotated Screenplay* (New York: Inventory Press, 2019).

11   https://worldstarhiphop.com/videos/videoc.php?v=wshhRQ6J0h mH0Oq0C4P2#comments-arena. Accessed on June 15th, 2021.

12   https://www.nytimes.com/2020/02/06/movies/oscarssowhite-history.html.

13   One thinks of Gaspar Noe's *I Stand Alone (Seul Contre Tous)* (1998) or *Irréversible* (2002) where the violence is reprehensible but occurs under conditions that could be deemed justifiable. Much is made of the post 9/11 atmosphere, but there is precedent in the continental horror films of the 1990s and 2000s.

14   Kerner, 24.

15   Ryan Poll, "Can One 'Get Out?' The Aesthetics of Afro-Pessimism," *Arts and Activism* 51, no. 2 (Fall 2018): 74.

16   Whether that be through material possession or control, or the placation of fears by assuming the identity of the thing that most inspires dread, which might explain why "blacking up" still occurs all too frequently around Halloween and other costumed celebrations.

17   Raengo, 75.

18   Hartman, 26.

19   In the way that a greek chorus in greek tragedies would offer warnings through premonition or declare the fate of characters in advance of events that would manifest their fate. The declaration is to Stay Woke, but one of the film's central tensions pivots on Chris' recognition that things seem strange in the Armitage residence and his desire to be with Rose.

20   Delgado and Stefancic, 2.

21   Sharpe, 21.

22   Sharpe, 9.

23   Poll, 89.

24 Recall how Chris notices that his cell phone is frequently being unplugged in an effort, unbeknownst to him until the very end, to breakdown his connection to others and the outside world.

25 Anne Anlin Cheng, "The Shell Game: From 'Get Out' to 'Parasite'" *Los Angeles Review of Books*, February 21, 2020: https://www.lareviewofbooks.org/article/shell-game-get-parasite/.

26 Cheng, "The Shell Game: From 'Get Out' to 'Parasite'."

27 Cheng, "The Shell Game: From 'Get Out' to 'Parasite'."

28 Wilderson, *Afropessimism*, 192.

29 Due, 12.

30 Yancy, xiii.

31 Cheng, "The Shell Game: From 'Get Out' to 'Parasite'."

32 Poll, 80.

33 Oluo, 2.

34 Sharpe, 15.

35 See "Poll: Can one 'Get Out?' The aesthetics of Afro-pessimism." In Poll's estimation, "If Chris is woke, then why does he not recognize that he is in the midst of a horror narrative until it is nearly too late? … For all of Chris's assumed awareness of structural and intstitutional racism, he still can't imagine the worst: that slavery remains active in the present and that Blacks remain marked as slaves," 80.

36 Wilderson, *Afropessimism*, 193.

37 See Bob Marley, "No Woman, No Cry" *Natty Dread* [album]. Label: Island/Tuff Gong; release date: October 25, 1974.

38 Ralph Ellison, *Invisible Man* (New York: Vintage International, 1995), 488.

39 Ellison, 3.

40 Yancy, xiv.

41 Hartman, 20.

42 This scene anticipates with remarkable precision the incident between A. Cooper and C. Cooper described earlier when A. Cooper says to C. Cooper, "I'm going to call the cops and tell them an African American man is threatening my life."

43 See Ibram X. Kendi, *Stamped from the Beginning: The Definitive History of Racist Ideas in America* (New York: Nation Books, 2016).

44 Wilderson, *Afropessimism*, 226.

45 Sharpe, 16.

Conclusion

1 Kevin Quashie, *Black Aliveness, or a Poetics of Being* (Durham: Duke University Press, 2021), 146.
2 Quashie, 146.
3 Quashie, 147.
4 https://nypost.com/2021/03/18/desantis-blocks-critical-race-theory-from-florida-classrooms/.
5 However, its success in generating immense profits for studios and investors surely offset any ideological opposition.
6 https://lareviewofbooks.org/article/humanities-age-loneliness/.
7 Wilderson, *Afropessimism*, 102.

FURTHER READING

Alessandra Raengo, *Critical Race Theory and Bamboozled* (Bloomsbury, 2016).
  An earlier entry in the Film Theory in Practice series, it offers an introduction to foundational debates and formative writings in critical race theory, then uses Spike Lee's *Bamboozled* (2000) to illustrate how critical race concepts can be turned to film analysis.

Christina Sharpe, *In the Wake: On Blackness and Being* (Durham: Duke University Press, 2016).
  By activating four metaphorical registers of the slave ship—the Wake, the Ship, the Hold, and the Weather—this book shows how the "afterlives of slavery" haunt Black life in the present from the carceral continuum of the prison industrial complex to atmospheres of Black death that designate the elimination of Blackness as normative.

Eric Lott, *Black Mirror: The Cultural Contradictions of American Racism* (Cambridge, MA: The Belknap Press of Harvard University Press, 2017).
  Cutting across a wide range of media and performance, this book explores the ingrained and contradictory dynamics of Black representations in "U.S. racism's theaters of fantasy." Lott shows how performances that endorse white identifications across lines of racial difference work to extend white hegemony, but also reveal the contradictions from which it draws its power.

Frank B. Wilderson III, *Red, White, and Black: Cinema and the Structure of U.S.Antagonisms* (Durham: Duke University Press, 2010).
  Through close readings of *Antwone Fisher* (Denzel Washington, 2002), *Bush Mama* (Haile Gerima, 1979), *Skins* (Chris Eyre, 2002), and *Monster's Ball* (Marc Forster, 2002), Wilderson challenges Hollywood cinema's capacity to accurately reflect US racial antagonisms.

Jared Sexton, *Black Masculinity and the Cinema of Policing*
(Switzerland: Palgrave Macmillan, 2017).
This book surveys representations of Black masculinity in
popular film and television series. It responds to a resurgence
of anti-Blackness in popular culture at the turn of the twenty-
first century that ran parallel to divergent neoliberal and
neoconservative desires to see images of Black masculinity
empowered to certain limits within the domain of the socio-
political or along the well-mapped inroads of organized athletics.
Sexton argues that these phenomena are not separate, but that
one is an extension of the other.

SUGGESTED FILMS AND MEDIA

Blacula (William Crain, 1972)
Ganja and Hess (Bill Gunn, 1973)
Scream Blacula Scream (William Crain, 1973)
Def by Temptation (James Bond III, 1990)
Candyman (Bernard Rose, 1992)
Tales From the Hood (Rusty Cundieff, 1995)
Scary Movie (Keenen Ivory Wayans, 2000)
Da Sweet Blood of Jesus (Spike Lee, 2014)
The First Purge (Gerard McMurray, 2018)
Random Acts of Flyness (Terence Nance, 2018)
Horror Noire: A History of Black Horror (Xavier Burgin, 2019)
Bad Hair (Justin Simien, 2020)
Candyman (Nia DaCosta, 2021)

INDEX

Locators followed by "n." indicate endnotes